OECD Green Growth Studies

Greening the Blue Economy in Pomorskie, Poland

This work is published on the responsibility of the Secretary-General of the OECD. The opinions expressed and arguments employed herein do not necessarily reflect the official views of the Organisation or of the governments of its member countries.

This document, as well as any data and map included herein, are without prejudice to the status of or sovereignty over any territory, to the delimitation of international frontiers and boundaries and to the name of any territory, city or area.

Please cite this publication as:
OECD (2017), Greening the Blue Economy in Pomorskie, Poland, OECD *Green Growth Studies*, OECD Publishing, Paris.
http://dx.doi.org/10.1787/9789264281509-en

ISBN 978-92-64-28149-3 (print)
ISBN 978-92-64-28150-9 (PDF)
ISBN 978-92-64-28401-2 (ePub)

Series: OECD Green Growth Studies
ISSN 2222-9515 (print)
ISSN 2222-9523 (online)

The statistical data for Israel are supplied by and under the responsibility of the relevant Israeli authorities. The use of such data by the OECD is without prejudice to the status of the Golan Heights, East Jerusalem and Israeli settlements in the West Bank under the terms of international law.

Corrigenda to OECD publications may be found on line at: *www.oecd.org/publishing/corrigenda*.
© OECD 2017

You can copy, download or print OECD content for your own use, and you can include excerpts from OECD publications, databases and multimedia products in your own documents, presentations, blogs, websites and teaching materials, provided that suitable acknowledgment of OECD as source and copyright owner is given. All requests for public or commercial use and translation rights should be submitted to *rights@oecd.org*. Requests for permission to photocopy portions of this material for public or commercial use shall be addressed directly to the Copyright Clearance Center (CCC) at *info@copyright.com* or the Centre français d'exploitation du droit de copie (CFC) at *contact@cfcopies.com*.

Foreword

This report was prepared by the Local Economic and Employment Development (LEED) Programme within the Centre for Entrepreneurship, SMEs, Local Development, and Tourism of the Organisation for Economic Co-operation and Development (OECD). It is an output from a project on boosting skills ecosystems for greener jobs carried out as part of the OECD LEED programme of work with support from the European Commission.

Managing the impacts of climate change is an unprecedented policy challenge that affects every aspect of the global economy. While policy makers at the national level increasingly grapple with coordinating an international response, it is at the local level that the true effects are felt, including the impacts of rising sea levels, more volatile and extreme weather events and worsening pollution and air quality.

Consequently, innovative policy solutions are often found locally, where many stakeholders have a role to play, including local governments, business, training providers, civil society, social welfare organisations, as well as universities. Strategies to make economic activities greener while furthering growth objectives are particularly important within communities undergoing structural changes as a result of digitalisation, globalisation, and climate change. Robust employment and skills strategies targeted appropriately can provide a mechanism to attract new investments and jobs in a more sustainable manner.

This report analyses opportunities to use coastal resources to grow the "blue" economy, which has emerged in recent years to encompass the sustainable economic development of oceans and coastlines. It highlights programmes and policies that have been introduced in Pomorskie, Poland, a dynamic coastal area with significant opportunities to leverage its distribution of natural resources. A key aspect of this study was the implementation of an employer survey to understand how local companies (especially SMEs) are greening their workplace practices, products and services. The results of this survey demonstrate that companies face many administrative and financial barriers to implement green measures within the blue economy.

This report shows that more can be done to articulate a shared vision for the green activities within the blue economy. Policy makers can also promote knowledge sharing in collaboration with business and leverage the use of the European Social Fund to provide more skills training opportunities that address skills shortages in the blue economy and provide pathways for people into greener jobs.

The Organisation for Economic Co-operation and Development remains committed to providing practical advice to further the transition to a green economy, including at the local level through its Local Employment and Economic Development (LEED) Programme.

This report was prepared by Nathalie Cliquot (OECD) and Angela Attrey (OECD) under the supervision of Jonathan Barr (Head of the Employment and Skills Unit within the LEED Programme) and Sylvain Giguere (Head of OECD LEED Division) with support from Michela Meghnagi and François Iglesias. Sections of the report were also drafted by members of an expert team composed of

Professor Iwona Sagan and Dr Grzegorz Masik (University of Gdańsk), Dr Tavis Potts (University of Aberdeen), and Dr Dean Stroud (Cardiff University). Thanks also go to Lindsey Ricker (OECD) for useful editorial support.

This project would not have been possible without the participation and co-operation from the Polish Ministry of Infrastructure and Development and the Marshal Office of the Pomorskie Voivodeship. In particular the Marshal Office hosted the project roundtable that took place in November 2014 in Gdańsk. The project and report benefitted from the active contribution from a steering committee: Przemysław Herman and Joanna Obarymska-Dzierzgwa from the Polish Ministry of Infrastructure and Development and Jan Dębicki from the Marshal Office of the Pomorskie Voivodeship. Finally, Piotr Klawsiuc and Anna Barczynska from the Centre for Social Research (PBS) contributed to the delivery of a company survey as part of the project.

Table of contents

Executive summary 9

Chapter 1. **Locally promoting green growth in coastal economies** 11
    Greening the economy: A local challenge 12
    The challenges and opportunities of greening coastal areas 13
    The concept of the marine economy is shifting to incorporate green elements . . 15
    Local strategies for greening coastal areas 17
    Conclusions 19
    References 20
    Further reading for Chapter 1 21

Chapter 2. **National and regional frameworks for greening blue economy sectors in Poland and Pomorskie** 23
    Understanding governance of the green and marine economy 24
    The Polish national regulatory framework for greening the economy 24
    Greening policies in regions, counties and municipalities 25
    A fragmented policy framework for marine economy sectors and water management activities 26
    Conclusions 31
    Notes 32
    References 32
    Further reading for Chapter 2 32

Chapter 3. **Greening the blue economy in Pomorskie** 35
    Overview 36
    Pomorskie: An attractive and dynamic Polish region 36
    Pomorskie has traditionally strong marine economy sectors 37
    Assessing the greening potential of marine economy sectors in Pomorskie 40
    Conclusions 53
    Notes 53
    References 53
    Further reading 54

Chapter 4. **Greening company practices and the impact on skills in the blue economy sectors** 57
    Most firms in Pomorskie consider environmental issues to pose minor challenges to their businesses 59
    Most companies have introduced green measures in their business practices . . . 60
    Regulatory compliance remains the main driver for greening business practices 60

Financial and administrative barriers are the most frequently mentioned
obstacles to greening practices. 61
The impact of greening on skills and jobs in the marine economy sectors:
need for technical skills. 62
The skills ecosystems: training providers and obstacles to training 64
How reactive is the training system to companies' needs? 65
Knowledge sharing activities remain limited. 65
Support needed from the public sector. 67
Conclusions 67
References 68

Chapter 5. **Skills ecosystem responses** 69
Overview 70
Pomorskie is a strong higher education centre in Northern Poland
with specialities in the marine economy sectors 70
Skills shortages (especially of highly technical skills) and difficulties
retaining talent have already emerged in marine economy sectors 71
The response of higher education institutions to the skills needs of the green
economy. 73
A limited response from public employment services, continuing education
and training programmes 75
Limited knowledge-sharing activities between education and businesses. 76
Conclusions 78
References 79

Chapter 6. **Policy recommendations** 81
Key recommendations. 82
Better articulating a vision for the green economy within marine economy
sectors 82
Assist businesses in seizing opportunities to green traditional as well as
emerging sectors. 85
Promoting skills and knowledge sharing in collaboration with businesses 88
Leveraging the European Social Fund to encourage employment and skills
development 92
References 93

Tables

3.1. Evaluation of the greening potential of blue economy sectors in Pomorskie
by interviewees 40

Figures

3.1. Structure of employment in the Pomorskie region and Poland (2012) 37
4.1. Size of the surveyed companies 58
4.2. Main economic sectors of the surveyed companies. 59
4.3. Identified environmental challenges 60
4.4. Main drivers of greening measures in companies 62
4.5. Obstacles to green measures 62
4.6. Obstacles to green measures 63

4.7.	Most frequently required skills for implementation of green measures	63
4.8.	Skills ecosystems training providers	64
4.9.	Obstacles to training	65
4.10.	Activities requiring public sector support	67

Follow OECD Publications on:

 http://twitter.com/OECD_Pubs

 http://www.facebook.com/OECDPublications

 http://www.linkedin.com/groups/OECD-Publications-4645871

 http://www.youtube.com/oecdilibrary

 http://www.oecd.org/oecddirect/

Executive summary

As a coastal area on the Baltic Sea, Pomorskie faces unique challenges and opportunities associated with the transition to a green economy. This report focuses on the development of the blue economy, which is associated with sustainable development of the oceans and coastlines surrounding the region. While policy has evolved in Poland in congruence with increased European emphasis on low-carbon production, there has been increased fragmentation in the management of environmental and labour market policies at both the regional and national level. This is particularly true for the blue economy, where a variety of ministries are responsible for the management of different water resources and skills issues.

This report analyses the specific skills needed to support green growth in Pomorskie, Poland and how related labour market and training programmes can be made more effective in supporting the transition to a low-carbon economy. To better understand the needs of employers as well as how they view the green economy, the OECD implemented a survey to employers, predominantly from small and medium sized enterprises (SMEs). The results demonstrated that companies view advanced technical skills as well as entrepreneurial and interpersonal skills as particularly important for adopting greener practices in the workplace. However, companies face a variety of legal, social, and financial obstacles to greening their practices. Many company green measures have been driven by legislation and regulation from the government as opposed to corporate-led initiatives.

Pomorskie is a strong educational centre for the blue economy sector. Through the University of Gdańsk and the University of Gydnia, the higher education sector has played an important role in working with companies to organise training programmes and specialised curricula for the blue economy sectors. Despite these efforts, the region faces challenges in retaining talent because of the low wages on offer relative to neighbouring OECD countries. A mixture of transversal and specific skills is needed in Pomorskie to further support the development of the blue economy. A number of key recommendations emerge from this report.

Key recommendations

Better articulate a vision for marine economy sectors

An overall vision for the development of greener activities should be articulated. Through this process, the governance and decision-making framework related to the management of water and the use of water assets should be streamlined to minimise the administrative burden and bureaucratic delay associated with the transition to a green economy. As part of this exercise, partnerships should be established with other OECD countries using existing international governance mechanisms, such as the European multi-sectoral maritime stakeholder platform for the Baltic Sea. Local policy makers could further harmonise the management and co-ordination of activities related to water assets, such as the seabed or shoreline of Pomorskie. Through a strategic over-arching vision, assistance could also be given to businesses and employer groups to further develop an integrated strategy to develop clusters related to the marine (blue) economy.

Assist businesses to seize opportunities to green traditional and emerging sectors

The company survey conducted in Pomorskie found that the majority of businesses do not consider environmental issues to be a significant threat or challenge for their businesses. Similarly, businesses note that "greening" production remains a legally demanding and cumbersome process. Providing more targeted assistance to SMEs and raising awareness amongst the private sector could help to "future-proof" local industries in Pomorskie. Initiatives to support entrepreneurship and innovation in the blue economy could also be of assistance.

Promote skills and knowledge-sharing in collaboration with businesses

Pomorskie has a significant education and training infrastructure that already offers some specialised courses for environmentally sustainable production and the blue economy. However, collaboration between different stakeholders in the training landscape is weak, and there are few formalised partnerships between businesses, research institutions and the education and training sector. Ensuring that the skills demanded by businesses are included in training curricula through formal governance mechanisms is an essential first step to addressing this issue. Promoting awareness of green issues and diffusing innovation throughout the skills ecosystem is also important for furthering the transition to a green economy.

Leveraging the European Social Fund to encourage employment and skills development

Pomorksie has the option of utilising European funds to build skills in green sectors. There is a strong precedent for the use of shared European funding for green apprenticeships and related training mechanisms. These funds could also be used to expand the capacities of the Polish public employment service to build the skills needed for sustainable production in the future.

Chapter 1

Locally promoting green growth in coastal economies

Human activity is placing significant stress on the environment, which will have long-term social and economic implications. This chapter discusses the rationale for developing local strategies, which support the transition to a greener economy. To consider these local strategies, this chapter considers the challenges coastal areas face in actualizing a greener economy. Despite these barriers, opportunities for marine industries provide ample justification for the shift to a greener economy. In particular, this chapter analyses the opportunities for coastal regions to develop "blue" economies, which promote sustainable economic development and job creation in a marine environment. International examples are provided to demonstrate how the concept of the blue economy is incorporated within local development strategies. These examples highlight global trends in the marine economy along with strategies for promoting blue growth. Through this comprehensive perspective, these examples offer strategies that are pertinent to other marine economies throughout the world, including Pomorskie.

Greening the economy: A local challenge

While most economies continue to strive for economic growth, it is now widely recognised that economic development is placing unsustainable pressures on the environment. Thus, there are increasing calls for the greening of economies. A green economy can be defined as an economy that fosters economic growth and development while ensuring natural assets continue to provide the resources and environmental services on which well-being relies. This entails catalysing investment and innovation, ensuring that natural assets can deliver their full economic potential in a sustainable way, including the provision of critical services – clean air and water, and the resilient biodiversity needed to support food production and human health (OECD, 2011).

Reducing the impact of economic production and consumption on the environment will require a transformation in the way that people live and work, and local actors can play an important role in driving forward this transformation. Promoting a green economy as part of sustainable and equitable development has therefore become the focus of a number of countries and local governments. For example, the European Union's Europe 2020 strategy document aims to reduce greenhouse gas emissions to 20% below 1990 levels (and up to 30% below, under the right conditions), produce 20% of energy from renewables and ensure a 20% increase in energy efficiency (European Commission, 2010). Such targets sit alongside its plans for inclusive growth, which seek "to modernise labour markets and empower people by developing their skills" along with the greening of work more specifically reflected in the "Resource Efficient Europe" and "An Agenda for New Skills and Jobs" initiatives (European Commission, 2010).

Action on transitioning towards a green economy is required at all levels. "Top-down" (national and supra-national) policy imperatives – such as those discussed in the Europe 2020 strategy document, as well as state-driven initiatives – provide a blueprint for change, but critical to driving forward transformation and realising efforts to green activities is developing the necessary participatory frameworks and mechanisms at the local and regional level. Regions and localities are embedded within state-centric models of institutional control, and subject to extensive networks of governance. Such patterns of governance shape decision-making capacities for economic development in important ways and play a critical role in the positioning of social actors in transition efforts (Pierre, 2014). Capacity for "bottom-up" delivery of green economic development at the local level reflects the existing patterns of interaction between state and local institutions and societal partners (Stroud et al., 2014).

The co-ordination of responses between governments, businesses and employers is imperative for action on climate change to be effective with the transformation of regions enabled where co-productive partnerships are developed at the local level (Beer and Clower, 2013; Miranda and Larcombe, 2012; Miranda et al., 2011; and Stroud et al., 2014). Regional and local economies comprise distinct industries, households and infrastructure networks, and it is the particular pattern and nature of economic activities and networks that determine the potential for greening activity (Miranda and Larcombe, 2012; Miranda et al., 2011). Some regions, for example, are characterised by industries (e.g. heavy manufacturing and mineral extraction) that are significant producers of carbon emissions, and these regions will face greater challenges than others. More particularly, it is the way innovative capacities, business networks and skills are clustered within regions and localities, which remain important for the generation and diffusion of new technologies and practices, and thus opportunities for the "greening" of the local/regional economy (Miranda and Larcombe, 2012; Miranda et al., 2011).

Efforts to transition to a green economy carry the potential for developing new jobs and enhancing the skills base of the region/locality (particularly where the aforementioned clusters are organised to facilitate development in this direction), but at the same time, net job-losses might ensue (Bowen, 2012). In many ways there is a contradiction between developing sustainable jobs for a sustainable low-carbon economy and maintaining current employment levels; these moves may require lower levels of production and a dampening of demand for some commodities (Stroud et al., 2014). Hence, where significant levels of unemployment exist within a locality, societal partners may decide policies aimed at job creation of any kind is in the interests of the region (Bowen, 2012). Such perspectives are reinforced by the difficulties some localities may experience attracting sustained investment to support the transition to a green economy, which might be underscored by skills shortages and limited awareness – particularly among SMEs – of future needs for green skills and investments in training. Thus, whilst training needs at the local level might not differ markedly from needs in the wider national economy, regional and local authorities have a key role in linking societal partners and facilitating skills development responses that support such a transition (Martinez-Fernandez et al., 2013a).

The challenges and opportunities of greening coastal areas

In the context of promoting a transition towards a green economy, coastal areas present certain complexities and opportunities. They are attractive places to live and work, with half the world's population living within 60 km of the sea, and three-quarters of all large cities located on the coast. Coastal areas are also environmentally sensitive and are highly impacted by climate change, rising sea levels and the loss of biodiversity. They offer unique opportunities to build on their natural advantages to promote the transition towards a green economy emerging from traditionally strong blue economy sectors.

Coastal areas face unprecedented environmental challenges. Marine ecosystems are deeply impacted by climate change. Global averages of land and ocean surface temperature data show a warming of 0.85°C (0.65-1.06 °C) over the period 1880-2012, with current trends suggesting that a 4°C rise is likely by the end of the century (IPCC, 2014). Global sea levels have risen by 20 cm since the 1880s with the rate of increase rising to 3.2 mm per year (Church and White, 2011). The oceans are gradually acidifying due to absorbing a third of CO_2 emissions (UNEP et al., 2012) with unforeseen impacts on the calcification of organisms, habitats and food chains (Lough and Hobday, 2011). Hoegh-Guldberg & Bruno (2010) warn that coral reefs, seagrass beds and mangroves could disappear if ecological thresholds are exceeded. Coastal "squeeze" may occur in populated areas where infrastructure could prevent the migration of coastal habitats and undermine ecosystem services including carbon sequestration, nursing grounds for fisheries and storm protection.

Besides this marine component, coastal areas are linked to river basins and freshwater resources through a variety of natural and socio-economic processes. The cycle of water, sediment transport and human activities in the river basin (e.g. waste effluents) affects water quality and quantity and ultimately sea water quality. This impacts coastal ecosystems and human activity in coastal zones (fishing, aquaculture, tourism and recreation opportunities). Plastic littering is also a concern in terrestrial and marine environments. One study illustrates that within all marine litter, plastic accounts for 50-80% where it accumulates and concentrates in the convergence zones of the five subtropical ocean gyres (Barnes et al., 2009). By one estimate, 4.8-12.7 million tonnes of plastic waste generated annually in 192 coastal countries are entering the oceans, where it can harm wildlife and, once fragmented into small pieces, enter food chains (Jambeck et al., 2015).

At the same time, coastal areas offer unique opportunities to promote the transition towards a green economy. They can build on natural advantages and new sectors can emerge from traditionally strong maritime sectors, thus leveraging the skills and know-how of local workforces. This includes the transformation of traditional industries such as fisheries, shipping and coastal infrastructure, many of which are in decline or have experienced prolonged periods of economic crisis. It also includes the emergence of new maritime industries such as marine renewable energy, aquaculture and eco-tourism; and strengthening the links between productive and healthy ecosystems and sustainable local economies (UNEP et al., 2012; APEC, 2014). A number of regional, national and international strategies have emerged in recent years which call for the increased development of marine and coastal systems. Underlying this modernisation is the development of skills and innovation strategies that facilitate the transition (Potts 2010; 2011). Regional authorities in some coastal areas, such as the south-west region of the UK, for example, have made "green" development a priority, with a growing number of people employed in the energy efficiency and energy renewable sectors (see Box 1.1).

Box 1.1. **The Wave Hub, UK**

The economy of the South-West region of the UK is largely reliant on services (particularly tourism). It is an area that lags behind the UK in terms of productivity and economic growth and different parts of the region have been designated as either "less developed" or "transition" areas. The less developed areas of the region are in receipt of EU funds to aid regeneration and growth activities. More recently, strategies have focused on the green transition - numerous regional development policy documents are centred on the issue of green development, jobs and skills. The region is also home to a number of tertiary and higher education institutions, some of which are acknowledged specialists in sustainability. Alongside the growing number of environmental SMEs in the region, this provides the area with a competitive advantage in sustainable development.

The Wave Hub is one initiative emerging out of this regional context, which aims to produce electricity through wave and tidal power – the region's coast line has optimum conditions for this type of energy generation. Wave Hub is a private company owned by the UK Government, and funded in part by European Regional Development Fund (ERDF). A parallel development is the Peninsula Research Institute in Marine Renewable Energy (PRIMaRE), which was supported at its outset by the now defunct Regional Development Agency (now Local Enterprise Partnerships – LEPs) and led by the Universities of Exeter and Plymouth. Efforts to transition the region with initiatives such as Wave Hub have been principally focused on state led policy development – including with regard to necessary skills development, but LEPs aim to strengthen engagement with local business and local authorities.

Source: Wave Hub Limited, 2015.

Local and regional actors have a key role to play in developing coherent policies and strategies to support the transformation of local/regional economy in these places (Agarwal, 2005). More particularly, the quality of the jobs is enhanced at the local level when labour market institutions, the education and training system and the industry communicate regularly, as well as when social partners (notably trade unions) are involved in the process of transformation (Martinez-Fernandez et al., 2013a; Martinez-Fernandez et al., 2013b).

The concept of the marine economy is shifting to incorporate green elements

The concept of the marine or "blue" economy has emerged in recent years to encompass the sustainable economic development of the global oceans and coasts and reflects increasing state interests in maritime affairs. Broadly speaking, blue growth is seen as increasingly important at the national level, contributing between 1-5% on average to national GDP (Park and Kildow, 2014). For example, the Irish Integrated Marine Plan estimated that the global ocean market is valued at approximately EUR 1.2 trillion per annum, contributing approximately 2% to the world's GDP (Irish Government, 2012). This breaks down as marine services (e.g. tourism, shipping, ports) contributing the largest proportion at EUR 786 billion; marine resources (seafood, oil and gas, renewable energy) contributing EUR 337 billion and marine manufacturing (marine equipment, shipbuilding, and biotechnology) contributing EUR 96 billion.

With the blue economy concept, the focus often remains on the overarching objective of maritime growth rather than fostering a transition towards a green economy. Sectors such as traditional mineral exploitation for fossil fuels, ocean mining, coastal development, infrastructure and existing fishing practices are not considered to substantially contribute to the green economy or require a cleaner production transformation (Potts, 2010). Nevertheless, some blue economy strategies break the mould of the "business as usual development" model. Such strategies move away from the oceans being perceived merely as a means of resource extraction and deposition towards incorporating values around sustainable development. This includes addressing equity in access to, development of, and sharing of benefits from marine resources; developing green economic sectors that are innovative, jobs rich, low carbon and low impact; and integrating conservation biodiversity and ecosystem services into development models.

Recent policy shifts indicate that a "greener" blue economy will be the model that attracts policy support and investment both in advanced and emerging economies (see Box 1.2). For example, Europe is investing in the blue economy through its Integrated Maritime Policy (IMP) and the European Commission has released a Communication on the Blue Economy (EC, 2012) that identifies key sectors in renewable energy, aquaculture, tourism, mineral resources, and biotechnology. The EU perspective is that the blue economy offers ways to help steer the EU out of economic crisis by "investing in new sources of growth whilst safeguarding biodiversity" (EC, 2012). It recognises, alongside investing in new growth sectors, the key role of eco-innovation in driving cleaner production and delivering environmental benefits to existing sectors. The EU argues that the seas and oceans are drivers for the European economy and have great potential for growth that is smart, sustainable and inclusive.

In Southeast Asia, organisations such as PEMSEA (Partnerships in Environmental Management in the Seas of East Asia) and APEC are advocating stronger links between the

> **Box 1.2. Integrating green economy elements into the blue economy**
>
> Extensive and varied definitions and terminology exist for economic activity – both private and public – that occurs in the oceans. These include the blue economy, blue growth, marine economy, ocean economy, and the blue-green economy. Blue economy definitions are ambiguous as to the extent of the influence of the green economy or sustainability principles within the respective strategies.
>
> In many instances, national reporting systems are monitoring the economic and employment contributions of maritime sectors as a whole, including both traditional extractive and manufacturing activities, "the brown economy" and emerging "green economy" uses of marine environments and resources (for example in the US State of Ocean and Coastal Economies [NOEP, 2014]). The oceans are conceived as development spaces where the emerging spatial planning and strategic initiatives plan and integrate existing activities (oil and gas, fisheries, shipping, infrastructure) with emerging sectors (renewable energy, aquaculture, tourism). On the other side, some blue economy strategies move away from perceiving oceans as a mere means of resource extraction and deposition and instead incorporate values around sustainable development. This includes addressing equity in access to, development of and sharing of benefits from marine resources; developing green economic sectors that are innovative, low carbon and low impact; and integrating conservation biodiversity and ecosystem services into their models. Definitions across countries vary and include:
>
> - USA – the concept of the ocean economy derives from the ocean (or Great Lakes) and its resources being a direct or indirect input of goods and/or services to an economic activity: a) an industry whose definition explicitly ties the activity to the ocean, or b) which is partially related to the ocean and is located in a shore-adjacent zip code (NOEP, 2014).
> - UK – the blue economy encompasses activities which involve working on or in the sea. Also those activities that are involved in the production of goods or the provision of services that will themselves directly contribute to activities on or in the sea (Pugh, 2008).
> - Ireland – the blue economy is described as "economic activity which directly or indirectly uses the sea as an input" (Irish Government, 2012).
> - South Korea – the blue economy includes activity that takes place in the ocean and activity which uses ocean resources as an input (Park and Kildow, 2014).
> - The European Commission – describes Blue Growth as the long term strategy to support sustainable growth in the marine and maritime sectors as a whole. Seas and oceans are drivers for the European economy and have great potential for innovation and growth. Focus sectors include aquaculture, blue energy, tourism, and deep sea minerals (EC, 2012).
> - The United Nation Commission for Sustainable Development (UNCSD) states: "We consider the green economy in the context of sustainable development and poverty eradication as one of the important tools available for achieving sustainable development. […] We emphasise that it should contribute to eradicating poverty as well as sustained economic growth, enhancing social inclusion, improving human welfare and creating opportunities for employment and decent work for all, while maintaining the healthy functioning of the Earth's ecosystems" (United Nations General Assembly, 2012).
> - The United Nations Environment Programme (UNEP) – a green economy in the blue world is one that "improves human well-being and social equity, while significantly reducing environmental risks and ecological scarcities" and means creating sustainable jobs, lasting economic value and increased social equity (UNEP et al., 2012).

green and blue economies. In July 2012, PEMSEA hosted its congress "Building a Blue Economy: Strategy, Opportunities and Partnerships in the Seas of East Asia" and APEC established a Marine Sustainable Development Centre in Xiamen, China. The 2014 Xiamen Declaration from the APEC Ocean related Ministerial Meeting recognised the "linkages between Blue Economy, sustainable development and economic growth, in particular, the close linkage to ocean and coastal conservation efforts, innovative development, and economic reform and growth" (APEC, 2014).

Local strategies for greening coastal areas

Promoting the transition of coastal areas to a green economy requires integrated strategies that link policy delivery mechanisms such as marine planning, river basin management, individual sector plans, biodiversity conservation and societal engagement. This calls for regionally focused innovation systems, built upon regional specialisations that draw upon "blue" ecosystems including marine and inland water ecosystems as well as associated services, coastal infrastructure and human capital.

Sector development

Local economic strategy and policy instruments should actively facilitate and advance emerging sectors that offer high potential for eco-innovation, employment, and investment and relate directly to climate mitigation and adaptation. This includes growth sectors such as marine renewable energy (wind, wave, tidal, hydro power), eco-tourism; low carbon food and biomass production (particularly aquaculture); green infrastructure (e.g. ports), and green transport and logistics. An example of a key sector emerging in Europe is offshore wind. Around the world, offshore marine renewable energy has become a significant player. The sector is particularly important in Europe with investment, construction and expansion in the offshore wind sector aiming to provide a significant contribution to European energy demands. Several European countries are embracing wind for renewable energy production, including the Netherlands, Denmark, Sweden, Germany, the United Kingdom, and Ireland who are installing large amounts of capacity around the North Sea, the North East Atlantic and the Baltic Sea. In 2013, 418 new offshore wind turbines, in 13 wind farms, worth between EUR 4.6 billion and EUR 6.4 billion were grid connected with a total of 1 567 MW of capacity (EWEA, 2014). To date over 2 080 offshore turbines have been installed and grid connected in 11 European countries with a cumulative total of 6 562 MW across 69 wind farms concentrated in the North Sea and Baltic Sea regions (EWEA, 2014). Future projections are ambitious with forecasts of 40 GW of offshore wind power by 2020 meeting 4% of the EU's total electricity demand. Canadian provinces provide a good example of regional efforts to move towards a low carbon blue economy.

Box 1.3. Blue Economy Development in Canada: A provincial driving force?

Canada has a massive ocean estate that covers approximately 7.1 million square kilometres. Three ocean basins exist in the country: the Pacific seaboard; the Arctic seaboard and the Atlantic seaboard. Overall, Canada's ocean jurisdiction is regulated by the Oceans Act (1996). The Act is founded on the principles of sustainable development, integrated management and the precautionary approach. Canada was the first country in the world to adopt oceans legislation to protect, develop and manage the ocean estate.

> **Box 1.3. Blue Economy Development in Canada: A provincial driving force?** *(cont.)*
>
> In 2011, 315 000 people were employed in maritime industries in Canada with a GDP contribution of CA$ 38 billion (Maritime Sector in Canada, 2014). The main sectors are oil and gas, public services (e.g. defence), fishing, tourism and aquaculture. Under the Oceans Act a regional planning has been established in several sites. Large Ocean Management Areas (LOMAs) focus on areas under pressure from human activities to address conservation challenges.
>
> In Canada, provinces are an important driving force for blue economy developments. For instance, in Nova Scotia, the 2010 Renewable Electricity Plan commits the province to 25% renewable energy by 2015 and 40% by 2020. Tidal energy in the Bay of Fundy is developing as a key sector, with substantial energy resources identified. The Fundy Ocean Research Centre for Energy (FORCE) has estimated that 2 500 MW of extractable power exists in the region. In 2014 underwater power cables with a capacity of 64 MW were laid in the Minas Passage with capacity to power 20 000 homes and establishing the project as the largest tidal transmission project in the world (FORCE, 2015). Wave energy is a further source of renewable energy, but the potential for energy generation varies according to the type of waves produced. Sheltered seas such as the Baltic have much less potential than coasts with exposure to the prevailing wind direction and long fetches e.g. the western coasts of Americas, Europe, Southern Africa and Australia/New Zealand (Heino, 2013). Other sectors such as aquaculture and fisheries make a significant regional economic contribution to local employment and investment. The aquaculture industry has approximately 350 sites in Nova Scotia with salmon, mussels and oysters the main cultivated species. In Nova Scotia the sector produced 8 748 tonnes of fish and seafood in 2013 with a value of CAD 54 million. The sector employed approximately 636 people in 2013.

Marine spatial planning and river basin management

Both instruments rely on integrated approaches rather than considering certain activities or sectors separately. For example, traditionally, areas of the ocean have been designated for specific activities and any development process (if one exists at all) tends to consider only objectives within individual sectors, without an overall vision for ocean space or how uses inter-relate. This approach fails to consider the picture as a whole and often misses important complexities, interactions, conflicts and trade-offs. It also fails to identify opportunities for co-location and development across sectors. While the conventional approach has been adequate for the management of single sector activities (e.g. fishing) the oceans of today and tomorrow are increasingly busy spaces of multiple activities with cumulative impacts increasing over time. Marine Spatial Planning (MSP) has emerged as a tool that attempts to rationalise the use of marine space and improve decision making in marine systems (European Commission Maritime Affairs and Fisheries, 2011). In 2014 the European Parliament and Council adopted a Directive on Marine Spatial Planning that creates a common framework for implementation across Europe. The Directive requires all coastal European states to develop MSP proposals according to a number of common requirements but allows for flexibility over the way plans are developed and delivered (European Parliament, Council of the European Union, 2014).

Conservation of natural capital and the quality of ecosystem services

Local strategies to green coastal areas should value and conserve natural capital alongside economic development by ensuring the quality and flow of coastal ecosystem services (Potts et al., 2014). Mapping coastal ecosystem services on a regional scale is a relatively new scientific endeavour and its inclusion in planning and decision making is practically non-existent. The emerging role of "blue carbon" is an important area for exploration, whereby coastal ecosystems such as mangroves and sea-grass sequester large quantities of CO_2 comparable to forest and soil storage on land. This offers opportunities for developing economies to structure economic activity around coastal biodiversity conservation. Several key coastal habitats such as mangroves, salt marshes and sea grass meadows have been found to fix carbon at a much higher rate per unit area than land based systems and be more effective at the long-term sequestration of carbon than terrestrial forest ecosystems. This carbon sequestration role re-emphasises the importance of maintaining, and where possible rehabilitating, such ecosystems as an opportunity for ecosystem climate mitigation.

Leverage of local know-how and skills

Local strategies to green coastal areas should emphasise that regions have unique endowments of natural and human assets that can be harnessed to promote the green economy. The concept of the "Natural Advantage" (Potts, 2010) identifies the central role of education, skills and innovation in regional policy development. In coastal regions, the adaptation pathway will be different depending on the structure and interactions of economic, social, cultural, political and ecological systems. Potts (2010; 2011) identified that green economies tend to emerge from regional specialisations. In the coastal context this could include energy infrastructure, seafood production, ports, tourism and recreation. New opportunities exist in sectors such as marine renewable energy, ecotourism, aquaculture and coastal defence. However, such patterns of employment adjustment, involving skills acquisition, skills recognition and upskilling for the "greening" of existing industries, as well as for the development of new opportunities, must be premised on an understanding of the region in a number of ways – particularly with regard to existing skill profiles, the socio-demographics of the available workforce and the household composition and remuneration patterns that sustain households (see Fairbrother et al., 2012).

Conclusions

While they are crucial to economic activities, coastal areas face unprecedented environmental challenges. Marine ecosystems are deeply impacted by climate change and will require adaptation and mitigation intervention measures. Coastal ecosystems are also linked to inland water systems and river basins and can be impacted by upstream human activities. At the same time, coastal areas offer unique opportunities to promote the transition towards a green economy. They can build on natural advantages and new sectors can emerge from traditionally strong blue economy sectors, thus leveraging the existing skill sets and know-how of local workforces, whilst providing opportunities for reskilling to serve emerging sectors.

In this context, the concept of the "blue economy" is shifting from an approach focused on the economic growth and potential of maritime sectors towards an inclusion of sustainability aspects and green economy principles. Similarly, the potential of river basins and inland waters can be leveraged to further green the economy of coastal regions (e.g.

transport, ecosystems, and services for flood prevention). Facilitating the green transition calls for comprehensive local strategies. The objectives are to gear policy instruments towards the green agenda, to engage communities and businesses while addressing potential conflicts and trade-offs, and to align education and training policies to best prepare local labour markets for the green transition.

References

Agarwal, S. (2005), "Global Local Interactions in English Coastal Resorts: Theoretical Perspectives", *Tourism Geographies: An international journal of tourism space, place and environment*, 7:4, pp. 351-372.

Asia Pacific Economic Cooperation (APEC) (2014), *APEC Ocean-Related Ministerial Meeting Joint Statement, Xiamen Declaration - Towards new partnership through ocean cooperation in the Asia Pacific Region*, http://mddb.apec.org/Documents/2014/MM/AOMM/14_aomm_jms.pdf, (accessed 9 June 2017).

Barnes, D.K.A., F. Galgani, R.C. Thompson and M. Barlaz (2009), *Accumulation and fragmentation of plastic debris in global environments*, Philosophical Transactions of the Royal Society, B. 364:1985-1998.

Beer, A. and T. Clower (2013), "Mobilizing leadership in cities and regions", *Regional Studies, Regional Science*, 1(1) pp. 5-20.

Bowen, A. (2012), "Green Growth, Green Jobs and Labor Markets", *Policy Research Paper*, No. 5990 Washington, DC: World Bank.

Church, J.A. and N.J. White (2011), "Sea level rise from the late 19th to the early 21st century", *Survey of Geophysics*, Vol. 32, Issue 4-5: pp. 585-602.

European Commission (EC) (2012), "COM (2012) 494 Communication from the Commission to the European Parliament, the European Economic and Social Committee and the Committee of the Regions", *Blue growth -Opportunities for marine and maritime sustainable growth*, http://ec.europa.eu/maritimeaffairs/policy/blue_growth/documents/com_2012_494_en.pdf.

European Commission Maritime Affairs and Fisheries (2011), *Study on the Economic Effects of Maritime Spatial Planning: Final report*, Luxembourg: Publications Office of the European Union.

European Commission (2010),*EUROPE 2020: A strategy for smart, sustainable and inclusive growth*, Brussels, 3.3.2010 COM (2010) 2020 final.

European Parliament, Council of the European Union (2014), *Directive 2014/89/EU of the European Parliament and of the Council of 23 July 2014 establishing a framework for maritime spatial planning*, Brussels: Official Journal of the European Union.

EWEA (European Wind Energy Association) (2014), *The European Offshore Wind Industry – Key trends and statistics 2013*, www.ewea.org/fileadmin/files/library/publications/statistics/European_offshore_statistics_2013.pdf, (accessed October 17, 2014).

Fairbrother, P. et al. (2012), *Jobs and Skills Transition for the Latrobe Valley: Phase 1: Benchmark occupations and skill sets*, RMIT University and Swinburne University of Technology, ISBN 978-1-921-91673-1.

FORCE (2015), *The Bay of Fundy*, (online) http://fundyforce.ca/renewable-and-predictable/the-bay-of-fundy/ (accessed 9 June 2017].

Heino, H. (2013), *Utilisation of Wave Power in the Baltic Sea Region*, Finland Futures Research Centre, University of Turku, ISBN 978-952-249-272-2.

Hoegh-Guldberg, O. and J.F. Bruno (2010), "The Impact of Climate Change on the World's Marine Ecosystems", *Science*, Volume 328, No. 5985, pp. 1523-1528.

IPCC (2014), "Summary for Policymakers", *Climate Change 2014: Mitigation of Climate Change*, Contribution of Working Group III to the Fifth Assessment Report of the Intergovernmental Panel on Climate Change (Edenhofer, O., R. Pichs-Madruga, Y. Sokona, E. Farahani, S. Kadner, K. Seyboth, A. Adler, I. Baum, S. Brunner, P. Eickemeier, B. Kriemann, J. Savolainen, S. Schlömer, C. von Stechow, T. Zwickel and J.C. Minx [eds.]), Cambridge University Press, Cambridge, United Kingdom and New York, NY, USA.

Irish Government (2012), *Harnessing Our Ocean Wealth – An Integrated Marine Plan for Ireland*, www.ouroceanwealth.ie/publications.

Jambeck, J.R., R. Geyer, C. Wilcox, T.R. Siegler, M. Perryman, A. Andrady, R. Narayan and K.L. Law (2015), "Plastic waste inputs from land into the ocean", *Science*.

Lough, J.M. and A.J. Hobday (2011), "Observed climate change in Australian marine and freshwater environments", *Marine and Freshwater Research*, Vol. 62: pp. 984-999.

Maritime Sector in Canada (2014), *Maritime Sectors Gross Domestic Product by Industry 2006-2011*, www.dfo-mpo.gc.ca/stats/maritime/tab/mar-tab1-eng.htm.

Martinez-Fernandez, C. et al. (2013a), "Measuring the Potential of Local Green Growth: An Analysis of Greater Copenhagen", *OECD Local Economic and Employment Development (LEED) Working Papers*, No. 2013/01, OECD Publishing, Paris, http://dx.doi.org/10.1787/5k4dhp0xzg26-en.

Martinez-Fernandez, C. et al. (2013b), "Green Growth in the Benelux: Indicators of Local Transition to a Low-Carbon Economy in Cross-Border Regions", *OECD Local Economic and Employment Development (LEED) Working Papers*, No. 2013/09, OECD Publishing, Paris, http://dx.doi.org/10.1787/5k453xgh72ls-en.

Miranda, G. and G. Larcombe (2012), "Enabling Local Green Growth: Addressing Climate Change Effects on Employment and Local Development", *OECD Local Economic and Employment Development (LEED) Working Papers*, No. 2012/01, OECD Publishing, Paris, http://dx.doi.org/10.1787/5k9h2q92t2r7-en.

Miranda, G. et al. (2011), "Climate Change, Employment and Local Development, Sydney, Australia", *OECD Local Economic and Employment Development (LEED) Working Papers*, No. 2011/14, OECD Publishing, Paris, http://dx.doi.org/10.1787/5kg20639kgkj-en.

National Ocean Economics Program (NOEP) (2014), *State of the U.S. Ocean and Coastal Economies 201*, Centre for the Blue Economy, www.oceaneconomics.org/download/.

Parliament of Canada, (1996), *Oceans Act*, Ottawa: Minister of Justice.

OECD (2011), *Towards Green Growth*, OECD Publishing, Paris, http://dx.doi.org/10.1787/9789264111318-en.

Park, S.P. and J. Kildow (2014), "Rebuilding the Classification System of the Ocean Economy", *Journal of Ocean and Coastal Economics*, Vol. 2014 (4).

Pierre, J. (2014), "Can Urban Regimes Travel in Time and Space? Urban Regime Theory, Urban Governance Theory, and Comparative Urban Politics", *Urban Affairs Review*, published online 10 January 2014, http://dx.doi.org/10.1177/1078087413518175.

Potts, T., D. Burdon, E. Jackson, J. Atkins, J. Saunders, E. Hastings and O. Langmead (2014), "Do marine protected areas deliver ecosystem service functions that support human welfare?", *Marine Policy*, 14: pp. 139-148, http://dx.doi.org/10.1016/j.marpol.2013.08.011.

Potts, T. (2011), "The New Green Deal and KISA: A Global Perspective", pp. 186-214 in Martinez-Fernandez, C., Miles, I. and Weyman, T. (eds) *The Knowledge Economy at Work: Skills and Innovation in Knowledge Intensive Service Activities*, London, UK: Edward Elgar.

Potts, T. (2010), "The natural advantage of regions: Linking sustainability, innovation, and regional development in Australia", *Journal of Cleaner Production*, Vol. 18, No.8, pp. 713-725.

Pugh, D. (2008), "Socio-economic Indicators of Marine-related Activities in the UK Economy", *The Crown Estate*, p. 68, ISBN: 978-1-906410-01-8.

Stroud, D. et al. (2014), "Skill development in the transition to a 'green' economy", *Economic and Labour Relations Review*, 25(1), pp. 10-27.

UNEP, FAO, IMO, UNDP, IUCN, World Fish Center, GRIDArendal (2012), *Green Economy in a Blue World*, (Nairobi, Kenya: UNEP), www.unep.org/greeneconomy.

United Nations General Assembly (2012), *66/288. The future we want*, New York: United Nation Commission for Sustainable Development, p. 2.

Wave Hub Limited (2015), *Wave energy and tidal energy test site in Cornwall*, (online) www.wavehub.co.uk/ (accessed 8 June 2017).

Further reading for Chapter 1

Apollo Alliance (2008), *Green-Collar Jobs in America's Cities*, United States.

Caprotti, F. (2012), "The cultural economy of cleantech: Environmental discourse and the emergence of a new technology sector", *Transactions of the Institute of British Geographers*, pp. 3, 37, 370-385.

Gibbs, D. and K. O'Neill (2014), "The green economy, sustainability transitions and transition regions: a case study of Boston" *Geografiska Annaler: Series B*, Human Geography, pp. 3, 96, 201-216.

Hamdouch, A. and M.H. Depret (2010), "Policy integration strategy and the development of the "green economy": foundations and implementation patterns" in *Journal of Environmental Planning and Management*, 53, 4, 473-490.

Hassink, R. (2010), "Locked in decline? On the role of regional lock-ins in old industrial areas", Boschma, R. and R. Martin (eds.), *Handbook of Evolutionary Economic Geography*, Cheltenham: Edward Elgar, pp.450-468.

Kathijotes, N. (2013), "Blue Economy – Environmental and Behavioural Aspects Towards Sustainable Coastal Development", *Procedia – Social and Behavioral Sciences*, Vol. 101, p. 7-13.

Lawton-Smith, H. (2004), "The Biotechnology Industry in Oxfordshire: Enterprise and Innovation", *European Planning Studies*, pp. 7, 12, 985-1001.

Martinez-Fernandez, C., C. Hinojosa and G. Miranda (2010), "Greening Jobs and Skills: Labour Market Implications of Addressing Climate Change", *OECD Local Economic and Employment Development (LEED) Working Papers*, No. 2010/02, OECD Publishing, Paris, *http://dx.doi.org/10.1787/5kmbjgl8sd0r-en*.

Martinez-Fernandez, C. (2012), "Chile's Pathway to Green Growth: Measuring progress at local level", *OECD Local Economic and Employment Development (LEED)*, OECD Publishing, Paris, *www.oecd.org/cfe/leed/Green_growth_Chile_Final2014.pdf*.

Stocker, T.F. et al. (2013), "Technical Summary", *Climate Change 2013: The Physical Science Basis*, Contribution of Working Group I to the Fifth Assessment Report of the Intergovernmental Panel on Climate Change (Stocker, T.F., D. Qin, G.-K. Plattner, M. Tignor, S.K. Allen, J. Boschung, A. Nauels, Y. Xia, V. Bex and P.M. Midgley [eds.]), Cambridge University Press, Cambridge, United Kingdom and New York, NY, USA.

Strietska-Ilina, O. et al. (2011), *Skills for Green Jobs: A Global View*, Synthesis Report Based on 21 Country Studies, International Labour Office, Geneva, pp. 456.

Chapter 2

National and regional frameworks for greening blue economy sectors in Poland and Pomorskie

This chapter describes the key ministries and agencies in Poland who manage the legislative and regulatory framework for the green and blue economy. This institutional mapping provides a rich context for understanding where green and blue economy policies are designed, implemented and monitored throughout Poland. At the national level, both the Ministry of Economy and the Ministry of Environment have introduced a number of key policy directives related to the green economy. At the local level, voivodeships play a critical role in the implementation of many environmental policies and programmes. Within Poland, Pomorskie is positioned to provide substantial influence on the future of blue and green policies.

Understanding governance of the green and marine economy

Good governance is an essential enabler of green growth. To be effective, governments at all levels will need to work towards policy alignment and coherence. The Polish regulatory framework for greening the economy has deeply evolved in the past decade driven by EU membership and the use of EU funds to develop environmental policies, but also by a reshuffle of responsibilities for national strategic planning and for the delivery of key environmental policy instruments such as Environmental Impact Assessments (EIAs). Nevertheless, despite strong improvements in the past decade, there are concerns that Poland has not yet established a clear pathway to a greener low-carbon and resource efficient economy. However, change is underway – for instance, with the newly adopted law on renewable energy sources.

For the blue economy and water management sectors, the policy framework is rather fragmented. Strategic documents at the national and regional level do integrate green economy principles but strategies are more centred on socio-economic development of the sectors. In addition, the governance structure is complex, involving several ministries and administration bodies as each blue economy sector is addressed separately. This in turn undermines the implementation of spatial planning in maritime areas and inland waters, making it difficult to favour the co-development of economic activities such as tourism, offshore wind energy, seabed resources extraction, aquaculture or transport, manage conflicts between various sectors and place the green economy at the heart of activities.

The Polish national regulatory framework for greening the economy

The Polish national regulatory framework for greening the economy has evolved over the past decade. This evolution is reflected in the modification of the overarching framework of environmental policies. From the early 1990s to 2012, Poland's environmental planning framework was described in 4-year strategies, the National Environmental Policies (NEPs). NEPs gave a mandate to the Polish Ministry of the Environment to oversee implementation. This changed in 2009 when Poland introduced three overarching development strategies (long-term to 2030, medium-term to 2020 and the National Spatial Development Concept to 2030) together with nine strategic policies. The environment became part of the strategic policy on Energy Security and the Environment.

This strategy is overseen by the Ministry of Economy in co-operation with the Ministry of Environment. In 2011, Poland also started to work on a National Programme for the development of a low carbon economy. In 2011, a strategic document called Priorities of National Programme of Development of Low-carbon Economy*(Założenia Narodowego Programu Rozwoju Gospodarki Niskoemisyjnej)* was adopted. The document lists specific objectives related to low-carbon energy sources, energy and resource efficiency. Nevertheless, there have been concerns that the Polish pathway for transitioning to a green, low-carbon economy is not sufficiently defined within the strategy for Energy

Security and the Environment. Although the environmental performance of Poland has improved between 2003 and 2015, the Polish economy is still among the most resource and carbon intensive economies in the OECD due to its heavy reliance on coal (OECD, 2015).

Since Poland's accession to the EU in 2004, its environmental laws and policies have been largely driven by EU environmental law. The transposition of EU directives resulted in another 20 environmental laws and about 100 regulations. EU structural and cohesion funds have provided substantial support for the implementation of environmental policies. For instance, the Operational Programme Infrastructure and Environment 2014-2020 (*Program Operacyjny Infrastruktura i Środowisko 2014-2020*) from 2014 financed from two European funds – the Cohesion Fund and the European Regional Development Fund – offers support in complying with European standards for investments such as: constructing water works, sewage works, sewage treatment plants, modernisation of old landfills, constructing waste treatment and recycling plants, modernisation of heat and power stations, and modernisation of industrial plants in terms of environment protection.

The transposition of EU law in the Polish context is not always straightforward. After many years of debates and after the European Commission brought the case to the Court of Justice, the Polish parliament adopted a Law on Renewable Energy Sources in February 2015 to transpose the 2009 EU directive on Renewable Energy Sources (Directive 2009/28/EC). The new law establishes the rules and conditions for activities in the field of generating energy (electricity, biogas and biofuels) from renewable energy sources. The law aims to foster the development of wind, solar, biomass, and hydro energy and will contribute to stimulate the development of the green economy, i.e. creating jobs in the production, commissioning and maintenance of new installations. It also sets national targets for the renewable energy used in transport and in the gross final energy consumption. The law will also encourage energy generation by private citizens by simplifying their legal and administrative status and removing the need to meet the requirements of energy producers (who are considered to conduct economic activity by generating and selling electric energy). This law is an important step to foster investments in blue economy sectors and in particular in blue energy.

Greening policies in regions, counties and municipalities

In addition to the national framework, environmental policy implementation is largely the responsibility of sub-national authorities. Regions or *voivodeships* (whose self-government authorities are called marshals' offices) are responsible for some regulatory matters such as permitting and for setting investment priorities. In Pomorskie, for instance, the 2015 Regional Operational Programme for Pomorskie Voivodeship 2014-2020 (*Regionalny Program Operacyjny Województwa Pomorskiego na lata 2014-2020*), as a part of the investment priority on energy, provides for support of energy-efficiency, intelligent energy management and the use of energy from renewable sources in public infrastructure – such as public buildings – and in the housing sector.

Regional directorates that are subordinate to the Ministry of Environment are responsible for Environmental Impact Assessment (EIA) and Natura 2000,[1] the latter responsibility is also shared with State Forests. EIA is a process used to predict the environmental consequences (positive or negative) of a plan, policy, programme, or project prior to the decision to move forward with the proposed action. In the water sector, institutional arrangements are particularly complicated with seven regional water management boards while two rivers account for 97% of the territory. The co-ordination of the environmental governance system has long been identified as a key challenge. In 2008, the General directorate for environmental protection was established with headquarters in Warsaw and 16 regional directorates to streamline procedures for environmental permits and help facilitate the use of EU funds.

Together with the adoption of the EIA Act, this helped reduce time for issuing EIA decisions from 300 to 100 days. The management of EIA and Natura 2000 sites have been frequently mentioned by business representatives as strong administrative obstacles to the development of blue economy sectors in particular in the field of hydro-power and water transport. This indicates that there is still room for improvements and simplifications for instance with harmonised methodologies and better public participation in EIAs (OECD, 2015).

The National Environment and Water Fund (*Narodowy Fundusz Ochrony Środowiska i Gospodarki Wodnej*), the keystone of Polish environment protection and water management financing system, is also managed at the local level by regional officers. This fund is constituted by fees related to environmental protection such as fees for emission of dust and gases into the air, use of water from deep or surface sources, introduction of sewage into ground water, and waste storage. For instance, the Regional Environment and Water Fund in Gdańsk (*Wojewódzki Fundusz Ochrony Środowiska i Gospodarki Wodnej w Gdańsku*) finances environment protection and water management as a part of sustainable development and national ecological policy and ensures that the non-refundable European funds for environment protection and water management are fully used.

In addition to regions, counties (*powiats*) and municipalities (*gminas*) also have a role to play for greening the economy. Counties are in charge of secondary schools, social welfare, and multi-municipality infrastructure such as collective transport, roads, water supply, wastewater and waste collection. Municipalities are responsible for local development and spatial planning as well as since 2013, municipal waste collection and treatment.

A fragmented policy framework for marine economy sectors and water management activities

Blue economy and water management activities also depend on a separate, more fragmented policy framework not necessarily related to environmental policies. At the national level, the strategic documents guiding the development of these sectors are the responsibility of several ministries (regional development, agriculture and rural development and environment) (see Box 2.1). While the greening dimension is addressed, the core priorities rather focus on economic development.

With a sector approach (addressing each blue economic sector in a separate way), such national strategic documents result in the dispersion of responsibility and decision-making between several public institutions. This ultimately makes it more difficult to place green economy principles at the heart of activities as a holistic approach is necessary. This is visible in the difficulties in implementing spatial planning for Polish maritime areas. This issue is however currently being addressed. The Maritime Institute of Gdańsk is preparing a study of determinants of spatial planning of Polish maritime areas that will constitute the basis for the elaboration of the maritime spatial development plan. The

> **Box 2.1. Key national strategic documents for marine economy sectors and water management activities**
>
> The main strategic document is the **"Principles of maritime policy until 2020"**, which sets up a list of key priorities and objectives for blue economy sectors. The list of priorities includes developing education, maritime science and research, developing sea ports and means of their protection, facilitating maritime transport, increasing national energy security, sustainable development of sea fisheries, sustainable exploitation of the natural resources of seas and oceans, improving the state of maritime environment, protecting seashores, increasing maritime safety, as well as improving water management. The **"Marine Economy 2011"** document replaces this in a broader European context. It insists on the implementation of the EU's integrated maritime policy with a wide range of instruments such as maritime spatial planning, strategies for sea basins, and the so-called blue growth, i.e. short sea shipping, coastal tourism, maritime wind energy and desalination.
>
> National strategy documents for regional development also refer to blue economy developments and environmental protection. For instance, **"The National Strategy for Regional Development 2010-2020"** (*Krajowa Strategia Rozwoju Regionalnego 2010-2020*), prepared by the Ministry of Regional Development, is the keystone document of regional policy and mentions the development of water and wind energy, and the support of cluster development. It also refers to the importance of sea and inland navigation as green transport that impacts regional development. The National Spatial Management Concept 2030 (*Koncepcja Przestrzennego Zagospodarowania Kraju 2030*) goes a step further by specifying that maritime areas and coastal zones should be managed with integrated spatial planning with reinforced biodiversity and natural environment protection. It projects new forms of deriving benefits from maritime areas, through Renewable Energy Sources, mariculture[2] for ecological purposes or maritime tourism. The document also highlights the potential of water transport.
>
> The issue of rural areas, agriculture and fisheries in the context of water resources exploitation is addressed in the **"Strategy for Sustainable Development of Rural Areas, Agriculture and Fisheries 2010-2020"** (*Strategia Zrównoważonego Rozwoju Wsi, Rolnictwa i Rybactwa na lata 2012-2020*), which is issued by the Ministry of Agriculture and Rural Development. The document stresses the importance of:
>
> - sustainable development of agriculture, fisheries and forestry
> - actions aimed at reducing water pollution
> - diversification of electricity generation in rural areas
> - generating energy from renewable sources, especially agricultural biogas plants.
>
> The impact of climate change on the blue economy sector is discussed in **"The Strategic Adaptation Plan for Sectors and Areas Vulnerable to Climate Change Until 2020, with Prospects for 2030"** (*Strategiczny plan adaptacji dla sektorów i obszarów wrażliwych na zmiany klimatu do roku 2020, z perspektywą do roku 2030*). The document was prepared by the Ministry of the Environment and defines the objectives and the course of adaptation activities that need to be carried out until the year 2020 in the most vulnerable sectors and areas, such as: water management, energy sector, coastal zone and transport. As for the wind energy generation, the conditions are expected to deteriorate, i.e. more frequent long periods of windless weather or short periods with hurricane-strength winds. The observed and forecasted climate changes will have a significant, negative impact on the conditions in Polish coastal zones that may obstruct the functioning of maritime affairs through increased frequency and intensity of extreme phenomena. The most vulnerable parts of Polish coast are: Hel Peninsula, the central part of the Polish coast – especially the spits of coastal lakes – and the Vistula Spit.

> **Box 2.1. Key national strategic documents for marine economy sectors and water management activities** (cont.)
>
> **"The Indicators of Sustainable Development of Poland"** (*Wskaźniki zrównoważonego rozwoju Polski*), published by the Central Statistical Office (GUS), address the issue of fisheries. The document accentuates that "fish stocks protection implies ensuring sustainable exploitation" (GUS, 2011). The problem is, however, the fact that the majority of EU fishing fleets are too numerous in relation to the stocks available. In other words, reducing excessive exploitation of fish and maintaining balance in sea ecosystems is possible through actions aimed at limiting the size of these fleets. At the same time, the document calls special attention to the matter of economy's water-intensity, especially in case of industry, and to the expenditures on fixed capital dedicated to unconventional energy sources, such as rivers and wind.

spatial approach is demanding but is also a way of securing a holistic vision and incorporating a strong green dimension in the development of the blue economy.

The need for a holistic vision is further exemplified in the fragmentation that is visible in patterns of governance and co-ordination related to the use and management of inland waters. Spatial planning is undermined by an artificial division between water ecosystems (e.g. seabed and water column) and their use and management, which is a reflection of complex governance structures. For instance, the seabed is managed by the Polish Geological Institute while the water column is under the jurisdiction of Maritime Offices. The land (seabed) and water (column) areas thus fall under the responsibility of different units of administration, which creates fragmentation in planning for the greening of maritime activities.

At regional level, several strategic documents related to blue economy sectors refer to the socio-economic development while integrating sustainability and green economy principles. For instance, the possibilities of the exploitation of water resources for socio-economic developments are the central aspect of the Pomorskie Voivodeship Development Strategy or "The Territorial Contract 2014-2020".

Several studies were carried out related to the development of blue economy sectors sometimes in relation with the green economy (studies on Development Possibilities of Wind Energy Sector in Pomorskie Voivodeship, and Strategic Development of Small Ports and Marinas in Pomorskie Voivodeship). Strategic documents for the green economy such as the Regional Strategic Programme for Energy and Environment also touch upon blue economy sectors.

The Pomorskie region strategic planning regarding the blue economy and water management sector is comprehensive and much more territorially oriented than the national approach. The Pomorskie region approach may help to develop the national strategic planning of blue economy sectors development and Pomorskie may play a leading role in shaping the national policy in this field. Unfortunately, until recently, maritime areas were not subject to regional spatial planning. Only now actions were taken and a pilot study for the maritime spatial development plan conducted by the Maritime Institute of Gdańsk has been undertaken. The development and co-functioning of economic activities such as tourism, offshore wind energy, seabed resources extraction, aquaculture or transport within the limited area of national waters requires a spatial development plan,

> Box 2.2. **Key strategic regional documents for the development of blue economy and water management activities**
>
> *"The Pomorskie Voivodeship Development Strategy 2020"* (*Strategia Rozwoju Województwa Pomorskiego 2020*) identifies the key sea-related branches of economy and stresses the importance of development of regional touristic network products, such as small harbours and marinas. The Strategy calls attention to the chances for region's development through tightening its economic links within the Baltic Sea Region and the strengthening its position in the global economy.
>
> **"The Territorial Contract 2014-2020 for the Intelligent Development Operational Programme"**(*Kontrakt Terytorialny na lata 2014-2020 do Programu Operacyjnego Inteligentny Rozwój*) puts forward the idea of Pomorskie's local government for creation of the National Baltic Research Centre, as an element of the Pomeranian Knowledge Triangle initiative. It is thus possible to assume that research and education (especially higher education) related to key directions for regional economy (which includes maritime affairs) will receive strong support from the local government. They will also be treated preferentially as part of supporting companies' R&D.
>
> **"The Pomeranian Port of Creativity: Regional Strategic Programme for Economic Development"** (*Regionalny Program Strategiczny w zakresie rozwoju gospodarczego Pomorski Port Kreatywności*) is a fundamental document that highlights region's Baltic seaboard location, by lower Vistula, as an opportunity for economic exploitation of maritime resources. It lists, amongst others, innovative shipbuilding industry, commercially attractive maritime connections, maritime tourism. It also recognises that the collaboration within the Baltic Sea Region, within the framework of economic, administrative, cultural, social, technological, infrastructural, and educational links is essential for the region (Pomorski Port Kreatywności, 2013). The document stresses that Pomerania has the potential to become a prominent transport and logistics hub for Poland and the Baltic Sea Region, mainly thanks to the expected development of shipping connections. At the same time, the attention is called to the insufficient exploitation of Gdańsk and Gdynia sea ports that affects regional and national economy. This is partially due to largely complicated national procedures (such as customs) and the deficiencies of the transport infrastructure that connects the ports on land. The list of potential specialisations for the nearest future includes, amongst others, offshore technologies, which indicates that Pomerania clearly inclines to supporting sea-related branches of business.
>
> **"The Eco-efficient Pomerania: Regional Strategic Programme for Energy and Environment"**(*Regionalny Program Strategiczny w zakresie energetyki i środowiska Ekoefektywne Pomorze*) was adopted in order to create conditions for efficient regional energy and environment policy management until the year 2020. The document diagnoses the problems and challenges in the sectors of energy and environment. It points to the issue of *voivodeship's* deficit of energy sources, and also to its high potential for nuclear, gas, coal and renewable energy – such as offshore wind farms. The lack of certainty as to the nature of final determinations on national support mechanisms and the creation of distribution and control systems is considered to be the main barrier for renewable energy development. Therefore, the main scope of actions will include developing and modernising infrastructure, improving the quality network's development management as well as creating IT technologies for development and control of localised power generation.

Box 2.2. **Key strategic regional documents for the development of blue economy and water management activities** (cont.)

Since the natural attractiveness of coastal areas generates touristic attractiveness and high pressures from human activities on the environment, the document emphasises the importance of "protection of sea-related habitats and ecosystems, such as spits, cliffs, coastal lakes and species natural to the Gulf of Gdańsk, Bay of Puck and coastal waters of the Baltic Sea" (Zarządu Województwa Pomorskiego, 2013). Nevertheless, insufficient surface water monitoring causes the protective actions to be limited. Achieving a good status of water is possible through undertaking several actions, i.e. "sewage treatment and collection, providing adequate quality of drinking water, waste management, facilitating fish migrations in rivers and streams (by constructing of fish passes, etc.), actions aimed at reducing the impact of industry and agriculture on the waters, protection and preservation of ecosystems combined simultaneously with educational and organisational projects" (Zarządu Województwa Pomorskiego, 2013).

The document also describes the strategic initiative of creating the Mare Balticum Baltic Centre for Ecologic Information and Education – Climate Change Centre. The purpose is "the creation of an educational institution to promote knowledge on maritime ecosystems, environment protection, climate change, and sustainable development. The programme unites both, the *voivodeship* authorities and the academic society, through the participation of University of Gdańsk" (Zarządu Województwa Pomorskiego, 2013).

"The Study of Development Possibilities of Wind Energy Sector in Pomorskie Voivodeship"*(Studium możliwości rozwoju energetyki wiatrowej w województwie pomorskim)* analyses the issues related to wind energy and concludes that although the Baltic coast enjoys favourable conditions in term of wind energy resources, the process of locating wind farms encounters numerous obstacles that stem from insufficient information on favouring and limiting factors. Improving the development of wind power stations requires co-ordination due to, inter alia, possible spatial conflicts related to selecting installations' location and the terms of connecting them to the energetic system by high-voltage and EHV power lines. Nevertheless, Pomorskie Voivodeship has witnessed an increase of investors' interest in wind energy, which results in new investments in wind power stations. The energy produced at the offshore power stations will require a creation of transmission network to link it to the land energy grid. This, in turn, will require an analysis of means of laying the cables across the technical and coastal zones and other protected areas. The document points out the problem of passive policy of the majority of municipalities' authorities, who leave the matter of providing space for wind energy needs to investors and property owners. This situation should improve together with the introduction of development strategies for wind energy (Spatial Planning Office in Slupsk, 2003).

"The Study of Strategic Development of Small Ports and Marinas in Pomorskie Voivodeship" (*Studium rozwoju strategicznego małych portów i przystani morskich w województwie pomorskim*) is one of the determining documents for the development of maritime tourism. Its main objective is to establish the basic future functions of ports and marinas. The analysis in the Study includes the following stages:

- status quo diagnosis: Port and access infrastructure, property and land ownership, financial situation
- developmental determinants assessment: spatial, environmental, economic, and transport

> **Box 2.2. Key strategic regional documents for the development of blue economy and water management activities** (*cont.*)
>
> - identification of the potential of ports' specific functions: commerce and trans-shipment; industrial, fisheries, touristic, and others
> - definition of developmental recommendations: on the level of ports and marinas network, in relation to specific locations and local authorities.
>
> The results of the above mentioned analysis are that tourism will become the dominant industry in the future, with growth poles located in Łeba, Puck, Hel and Krynica Morska. Fisheries also seems to have high potential (chiefly in Ustka and Władysławowo) as well as other port functions in the areas with relatively high developmental potential for the tourism sector.
>
> The area of Gulf of Gdańsk was determined to be the growth centre, with growth poles in Hel, Puck, and Krynica Morska. Development in this area is forecast to stem from close proximity to the tri-city agglomeration and good communication infrastructure, including roads, railways and airports. The industry, commercial and trans-shipping activities in ports were judged to have the lowest development potential. The reactivation of the trans-shipping function is viable only in small ports of Ustka and Władysławowo, while only the port of Wałdysławowo and partially the ports of Ustka, Łeba and Hel were considered to possess the space or infrastructure for future industrial production.

as the conflicts between these functions may block their development. The potential conflicts between such activities as seabed resources extraction versus aquaculture and tourism, transport versus aquaculture and tourism, offshore wind energy versus transport are only the easiest to predict conflicts. To stimulate and intensify the blue economy development the scope of regional planning in coastal regions should be extended on the coastal sea which is now under the national level control.

Conclusions

The Polish national and regional frameworks for addressing the greening of the economy have deeply evolved in the last decades and were boosted by EU membership and the availability of EU funding. Despite strong improvements, there are concerns that Poland has not yet established a clear pathway to a greener low-carbon and resource efficient economy. In this context, the newly adopted law on renewable energy sources is likely to help secure investments in renewable energy and help reduce the country's dependence on coal.

For the blue economy and water management sectors, the policy framework appears fragmented. Strategic documents at the national and regional level do integrate green economy principles, but strategies are more centred on socio-economic development of the sectors rather than on the green transition. In addition, the governance structure is complex, involving several ministries and administration bodies as blue economy sector are often addressed separately.

This fragmented approach has so far been detrimental to the effective implementation of spatial planning for the blue economy and water sectors. Nevertheless, there are signs that Pomorskie is taking steps to improve this aspect by carrying out a study for the maritime spatial development plan. Pomorskie could play a leading role shaping national policy in this field.

Notes

1. Natura 2000 is an EU-wide network of nature protection areas established in 1992 to assure the long-term survival of Europe's most threatened species and habitats.
2. Mariculture is a specialised branch of aquaculture involving the cultivation of marine organisms for food and other products in the open ocean, an enclosed section of the ocean, or in tanks, ponds or raceways which are filled with seawater.

References

Biuro Planowania Przestrzennego w Słupsku [Spatial Planning Office in Slupsk] (2003), *Studium możliwości rozwoju energetyki wiatrowej w województwie pomorskim* [The Study of Development Possibilities of Wind Energy Sector in Pomorskie Voivodeship], Słupsk.

Central Statistical Office of Poland (GUS) (2011), *Wskaźniki zrównoważonego rozwoju Polski – SDI*, (Online) http://stat.gov.pl/cps/rde/xbcr/gus/Wskazniki_SDI.pdf (accessed 8 June 2017).

OECD (2015), *OECD Environmental Performance Reviews: Poland 2015*, OECD Publishing, Paris, http://dx.doi.org/10.1787/9789264227385-en.

Pomorski Port Kreatywności (2013), *Regionalny Program Strategiczny w zakresie rozwoju gospodarczego*, Gdańsk: Zarządu Województwa Pomorskiego.

Zarządu Województwa Pomorskiego (2013), *Regionalny Program Strategiczny w zakresie*, Gdańsk: Zarządu Województwa Pomorskiego.

Further reading for Chapter 2

Czarskiego, E. (2011), *Wskaźniki zrównoważonego rozwoju Polski* [Polish sustainable development indicators] Zespół pracowników Urzędu Statystycznego w Katowicach przy współudziale: Urzędu Statystycznego w Krakowie, Urzędu Statystycznego w Szczecinie, Departamentu Analiz i Opracowań Zbiorczych GUS [Statistical Office of Katowice in cooperation with: Statistical Office of Cracow, Statistical Office of Szczecin, Department of Analyses and Studies Aggregated Central Statistical Office], Katowice.

Gorzelak, G. (2000), *"Podstawowe pojęcia polityki regionalne"j, Departament Reform Ustrojowych Państwa w Kancelarii Prezesa Rady Ministrów, Municipium* ["Basic concepts of regional policy", Reforms of the State Department in the Prime Minister's Office], Warsaw.

Instytut Energetyki Odnawialnej, EC BREC IEO (2010), *Analiza możliwości rozwoju produkcji urządzeń dla energetyki odnawialnej w Polsce dla potrzeb krajowych i eksportu* [Analysis of opportunities for the production of equipment for renewable energy in Poland for domestic and export], Warszawa.

Międzyresortowy Zespół do spraw Polityki Morskiej Rzeczypospolitej Polskiej [Interdepartmental Group on Maritime Policy of the Republic of Poland] (2013), *Polityka morska Rzeczypospolitej Polskiej do roku 2020* [Maritime Policy of the Republic of Polish for 2020], Warsaw.

Ministerstwo Budownictwa [Ministry of Construction, Poland] (2007), Raport z wdrażania procesu Zintegrowanego Zarządzania Obszarami Przybrzeżnymi w Polsce (projekt), [Report on the Implementation Process of Integrated Coastal Zone Management in Poland (draft)], Warsaw.

Ministerstwo Gospodarki, Departament Doskonalenia Regulacji Gospodarczych [Ministry of Economy of Poland, Department of Economic Regulatory Improvement] (2012), *Ekspertyza dotycząca oceny propozycji z projektu III ustawy deregulacyjnej pt: Wydłużenie terminu na rozliczenie VAT w imporcie ze względu na skutki budżetowe oraz skutki dla prowadzenia działalności gospodarczej w tym rozwoju regionów nadmorskich* [Expertise concerning the assessment of project proposals III of the Act entitled deregulation: Extension of the deadline for settlement of VAT on imports due to the budgetary implications and consequences for doing business in the development of coastal regions], Warsaw.

Ministerstwo Infrastruktury [Ministry of Infrastructure, Poland] (2009), *Założenia polityki morskiej Rzeczypospolitej Polskiej do roku 2020*, Warszawa.

Ministerstwo Nauki i Szkolnictwa Wyższego (2015),*Program Rozwoju Kompetencji zastąpi kierunki zamawiane*, www.nauka.gov.pl/aktualnosci-ministerstwo/program-rozwoju-kompetencji-zastapi-kierunki-zamawiane.html (accessed 26 March 2015).

Ministerstwo Rozwoju Regionalnego [Ministry of Regional Development, Poland] (2012), *Koncepcja Przestrzennego Zagospodarowania Kraju 2030*, [National Spatial Development Concept, 2030], Warsaw.

Ministerstwo Rozwoju Regionalnego [Ministry of Regional Development, Poland] (2010), *Krajowa Strategia Rozwoju Regionalnego 2010-2020* [National Regional Development Strategy 2010-2020], Warsaw.

Ministerstwo Środowiska (2013), *Strategiczny plan adaptacji dla sektorów i obszarów wrażliwych na zmiany klimatu do roku 2020, z perspektywą do roku 2030*, Warsaw.

Spatial Development Plan for Pomorskie Voivodeship (2009), *Pomorskie Regional Studies*, Marshall's Office of the Pomorskie Voivodeship, Gdańsk.

Sejmik Województwa Pomorskiego [Pomorskie Regional Assembly] (2012), *Strategia Rozwoju Województwa Pomorskiego 2020* [Pomorskie Regional Development Strategy 2020], Gdańsk.

Strategia Zrównoważonego Rozwoju Wsi, Rolnictwa i Rybactwa na lata 2012-2020 (2012), Monitor Polski, Dziennik Urzędowy Rzeczypospolitej Polskiej, Warsaw.

Urząd Statystyczny w Szczecinie [Statistical Office in Szczecin] (2011), *Gospodarka morska 2011* [Maritime 2011], Szczecin.

Zarząd Województwa Pomorskiego [Management Board of the Pomeranian Province] (2013), *Regionalny Program Strategiczny w zakresie energetyki i środowiska Ekoefektywne Pomorze* [Regional Strategic Programme in the field of energy and environment eco-efficient Pomerania], Gdańsk.

Zarząd Województwa Pomorskiego [Management Board of the Pomeranian Province](2013), *Regionalny Program Strategiczny w zakresie rozwoju gospodarczego Pomorski Port Kreatywności*, Gdańsk.

Zaucha, J. (red.) (2009), "Planowanie przestrzenne obszarów morskich", *Polskie uwarunkowania i plan pilotażowy*, Instytut Morski w Gdańsku, Gdańsk.

Chapter 3

Greening the blue economy in Pomorskie

This chapter provides an overview of the key economic and employment trends in the Polish province of Pomorskie. This overview offers a context for understanding different nuances of Pomorskie's green and blue economy. It also describes Pomorskie's ability to develop more sustainable production processes in local industries within the blue economy. Barriers to "greening" the sectors related to Pomorskie's coastal resources are also examined.

Overview

The Pomorskie region is an economically well-developed region of Poland. The Tri-City metropolitan area forms a solid growth centre for the region. The post-industrial economic structure provides a good foundation for future dynamic development. The Pomorskie region is located in an ideal environment to offer innovative solutions that are necessary for the development of the green economy. The environmental conditions, together with the presence of the life sciences industry, create unique opportunities for the development of the region's green economy.

Pomorskie: An attractive and dynamic Polish region

Pomorskie is a *voivodeship*, or province, in north-central Poland with a diversified economy, growing population and significant natural resources. GDP has increased steadily since 2000 in Pomorskie, which aligns with trends at the national level in Poland. Unemployment was 6.8% in 2015, compared to a national average of 7.6%. Looking at the skills of the labour force, 30.5% had a tertiary degree in 2014. The national average was only slightly higher at 31%. These percentages have increased significantly since 2000, when only 12.3% of the national labour force in Poland (and 14.7% in Pomorskie) had attended university (GUS, 2014).

The Pomorskie region is situated on the coast of the Baltic Sea, by the Gulf of Gdańsk. It covers an area of 18 000 square kilometres with a population of approximately 2.3 million inhabitants. Its biggest cities are Gdańsk (around 457 000 inhabitants) and Gdynia (around 246 000 inhabitants). The metropolitan area, which includes neighbouring cities and rural municipalities, has a total population of 1.3 million inhabitants (GUS, 2014).

Pomorskie is one of the four regions in Poland (out of 16) that has a growing population (increase of over 100 000 inhabitants since 2003). The growth is generated both by a positive rate of natural increase and a positive rate of net migration. The real increase is around 2.5 per 1 000 inhabitants and is significantly higher than in the rest of the country (0.3 per 1 000 inhabitants) as well as many other regions of Central Europe. In spite of the population influx and relatively high birth rate (compared to the rest of Poland) the ageing population in the region is growing, while the working age population[1] is slightly decreasing. Nevertheless over the period between 2003 and 2013, the absolute number of working age people increased, which triggered a growth of supply within the regional labour market. In comparison to the national average, Pomorskie is characterised by a relatively young age structure and a low demographic dependency ratio (GUS, 2014).

The positive net migration rate in the Pomorskie region is partly due to the attractiveness of its labour market. Other main factors for the attractiveness of the region are the living conditions and quality of life, listed in various rankings as the best in Poland. When compared to neighbouring regions, and the more distant regions of north-eastern Poland, Pomorskie offers a significantly more attractive living environment. Nonetheless, it is not the entire region that offers new jobs for the migrant population – the large cities within the agglomeration are the most attractive labour markets. The city centres of Gdańsk and Gdynia are witnessing a high positive rate of migration and these trends also apply to their neighbouring districts. Over the period 2002 to 2010, the neighbouring districts of these agglomerations observed an average migratory inflow of over 5 per 1 000 persons.

The comparison of Pomorskie's employment structure with the rest of Poland reveals that agriculture is less prominent in the region than in the rest of the country. Sectors such as industrial processing, commerce, vehicle repairs, construction, transport and warehousing are relatively more developed in Pomorskie.

Figure 3.1. **Structure of employment in the Pomorskie region and Poland (2012)**

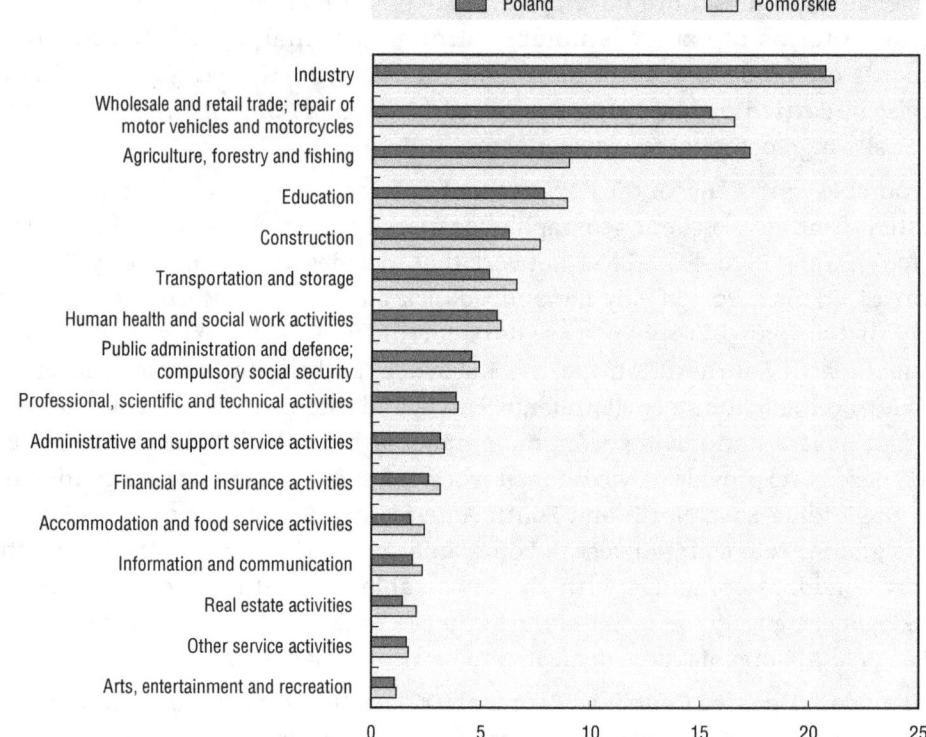

Source: Author's elaboration based on Central Statistical Office (GUS, 2014).

The level of education of the population is one of the important characteristics that define the economic potential of a given region or country, and it has specific implications for the potential greening of economic activity. An increasingly better-educated population is able to adapt to frequent changes in the labour market requirements through the acquisition of new skills and competencies. Therefore, the population's education level influences the potential possibilities of implementing new technologies or measures that benefit the environment. National Census data from 2002 and 2011 clearly indicate that both in the Pomorskie region and in Poland as a whole, the proportion of the population with higher education increased, while the proportion of the population with lower or no education decreased (GUS, 2014).

Pomorskie has traditionally strong marine economy sectors

Blue economy sectors are traditionally strong in Pomorskie. The Gdańsk Institute for Market Economics has identified shipbuilding, fisheries, and tourism as key sectors for Pomorskie's local economy. The importance of these sectors is also mentioned in the Pomorskie Voivodeship Development Strategy together with that of other well-developed sectors of Pomorskie's economy: sea-related industries, petrochemicals, electrical engineering, construction, wood and furniture, food. This strategy lists a number of significant sectors in Pomorskie, including sea-related industries, petrochemicals, shipbuilding, electrical engineering, construction, wood and furniture, tourism and food (Sagan et al., 2013).

Simultaneously, it is pointed out that the economic capabilities of maritime resources exploitation are gaining increasing prominence both within the region and in the context of a broader Baltic Sea Strategy. The Development Strategy lists maritime logistics, construction and repair shipyards, specialised shipyards, ship equipment providers and the offshore industry among the sectors that capitalise on the potential of Pomorskie's coastal location and that are developing particularly fast. Also, the position of yacht shipyards in terms of export is notably strong. The Analysis of Attractiveness for Investments of Pomorskie Voivodeship (*Analiza atrakcyjności inwestycyjnej województwa pomorskiego*), carried out in 2010, also listed logistics as one of the six sectors with exceptionally high potential for development.

Favourable conditions for the development of transport and logistics in the Pomorskie region stem from its excellent geographic location, i.e. on the sea coast and with direct access to the trans-European TEN-T network that includes: the A1 motorway, E65 railway line, Port of Gdańsk, Port of Gdynia, and Gdańsk airport. The region is also set on the crossing of two pan-European transport corridors: the VI corridor that connects Scandinavia with Southern Europe, via Katowice, and the IA corridor that connects Pomorskie and the Baltic states (Lithuania, Latvia and Estonia). There are two ports in the region that have a nationwide economic impact – the Port of Gdańsk, and the Port of Gdynia. These ports provide services for all types of freight, including to international ports in Asia, the Middle-East, North and South America and European ports like Rotterdam, Hamburg and St. Petersburg (Invest in Pomerania, 2014). The fact that the intersection of transport corridors coincides with the favourable, coastal location of Gdańsk (and Pomorskie) is also partly the result of the strategy of the Vision and Strategies around the Baltic Sea (VASAB) organisation, dedicated to maritime spatial planning.

The modern Deepsea Container Terminal (DCT) in the Port of Gdańsk, and the regular, weekly connections to Asia, operated by the world's largest container vessels, contribute to strengthening Gdańsk's position within the Baltic Sea region. It has become a key maritime port, from which goods are distributed by land transportation and smaller ships to other countries (Invest in Pomerania, 2014). In addition, the number of container terminals' global shipping connections in Gdańsk and Gdynia is expected to grow (Sagan et al., 2013).

In the years 2005-12 container trans-shipping in the Pomorskie region's ports grew in general terms from 470 170 units (2005) to 1.62 million units (2012), with a slight decline in 2009 (Invest in Pomerania, 2014). The Gdańsk Bulk Terminal, opened in 2013, is one of the largest among the Baltic ports, and boasts a trans-shipping capacity of up to 400 000 tonnes of products per year. Meanwhile, an investment started in 2014, will provide 20 storage tanks for petroleum and petroleum products with a total capacity of around 700 000 cubic metres for the Gdańsk Oil Terminal (Tarkowski, 2013).

Pomorskie Voivodeship Development Strategy projects a growth in demand for comprehensive transport and logistics services. "Containerisation and increasing inter-modality of transport, and sustainable development of cargo handling capacity and infrastructural facilities of Gdańsk and Gdynia ports will influence the strengthening of their competitive position on the Baltic market" (Sagan et al., 2013). Nevertheless, Gdańsk and Gdynia sea ports remain underexploited, due to overly complicated national procedures (customs) and insufficient transport infrastructure and port facilities. Similarly, the region's external accessibility and available storage capacities are also underexploited (in spite of significant investments in relevant infrastructure). This affects the competitiveness of Pomorskie's ports, limits their development possibilities and prevents the region from strengthening its position in the ports, transport and logistics sectors (Sagan et al., 2013).

Shipbuilding and maritime sector

One of the most prominent sectors in Pomorskie is the shipbuilding sector, which is concentrated in the area of Gdańsk and Gdynia. This sector includes the building, conversion, repair and decommissioning of ships and water vessels as well as the installation and repair of ship equipment. It also comprises activities in related sectors, such as metalworking, machines and tools. The sector has its own R&D infrastructure and facilities with specialised institutions such as the Ship Design and Research Centre, and the departments of the Technical University of Gdańsk and the Polish Naval Academy (Institute for Market Economics, 2008).

Altogether, the shipbuilding sector and related activities generate around 27 000 jobs, which amounts to 3.3% of all jobs in Pomorskie. Almost half of Polish shipbuilding sector entities are based in Pomorskie (Invest in Pomerania, 2014). Compared to the 1980's, shipbuilding activities are now more diversified and employ fewer workers. The place of the large, now-bankrupt shipyards of Gdańsk and Gdynia was taken by numerous smaller companies specialised in the construction of smaller vessels, the production of elements or the provision of other sea-related services. The sector is now primarily composed of six large local producers which are members of the Shipbuilding Association Forum Okrętowe (Gdynia Shipyard SA, Gdańsk Shipyard SA, Northern Shipyard SA, Wisła Shipyard Sp. z o.o., Gdańsk Ship Repair Yard SA, Repair Shipyard Nauta SA) together with an ample shipbuilding-related section of companies. It also includes small and medium shipyards that specialise in the production of sail and motor yachts, including high-end luxury vessels. In terms of yacht production, Poland is among the world leaders – in 2010 it was the world's second biggest yacht producer, surpassed only by the United States (Nietupski, 2010).

New specialisations were also introduced in the sector. Some shipyards switched to producing offshore industry vessels. Some started investing in the production of installations for the renewable energy sector. The European Commission (2012) notes that environmental and safety regulations, while seen as a significant challenge for the shipbuilding industry, can also be a major source of innovation and an important driver of blue growth for the sector. In terms of sales and production, the largest company, both on a regional and national scale, is the Repair Capital Group with its principle entity – Gdańsk Ship Repair Yard. The Group owns high-tech companies, such as IT-REM that specialises in advanced IT solutions for the maritime sector (Invest in Pomerania, 2014). Another important company is Remontowa Shipbuilding in Gdańsk. The company was awarded a contract for the construction of specialised cable-laying vessels for a Norwegian ship-owner in 2013 and is one of the world's top five leading shipyards of this type (Tarkowski, 2013).

Fisheries

Another sector recognised by the Gdańsk Institute for Market Economics in Pomorskie is the fisheries sector, comprised of entities related to fisheries, fishing and fish processing.

The fisheries generate over 8 000 jobs, approximately 20% of all of the jobs in the agro-food sector in Pomorskie. Pomorskie is responsible for 40% of the total employment in the fisheries sector in Poland. Companies within the fisheries and fish processing sectors are mainly located in coastal districts such as Puck, Słupsk and Nowy Dwór.

Tourism

Tourism is also a strong economic sector in Pomorskie, generating approximately 32 000 jobs, i.e. 4% of the region's total employment. The sector benefits from the natural environment (Baltic coast, Kashubian Lake District, Żuławy) and the region's history (Gdańsk, Malbork). The proportion of people employed in this sector is highest in the districts located directly by the Baltic Sea, i.e. Puck, Nowy Dwór, Lębork, the city of Sopot, and Słupsk. The proportion of people employed in tourism is relatively less important in the city of Gdańsk, the Puck district and the city of Gdynia (Invest in Pomerania, 2014). The sector fosters increasingly specialised forms of tourism, such as windsurfing, kitesurfing or deep-sea diving to explore wreckages from the Second World War. With traditionally strong blue economy sectors such as shipbuilding, fisheries and tourism, Pomorskie is ideally positioned to build on its strengths within these sectors to initiate the transition to the green economy. Besides the traditional sectors, there is also the potential for greening new and emerging blue economy sectors.

Assessing the greening potential of marine economy sectors in Pomorskie

To assess the green potential of traditional and new and emerging sectors, a series of 26 bilateral interviews were undertaken between March and October 2014 with representatives of academic society, business and regional authorities. Interviewees were asked to assess whether a sector had a high, medium or low potential for contributing to the green economy in Pomorskie. The table below presents the consolidated results of their subjective assessment. The majority of interviewees considered that the traditional blue economy sectors (shipbuilding, maritime transport, tourism) have the highest potential to contribute to greening Pomorskie's economy.

Table 3.1. **Evaluation of the greening potential of blue economy sectors in Pomorskie by interviewees**

Sectors	Level of "greening" potential
Shipbuilding industry	High
Maritime transport (including sea port development)	High
Maritime tourism, coastal tourism and cruises	High
Recreation and leisure	High
Medical services, spa	High
Renewable maritime energy resources	Medium/high
Blue biotechnology	Medium/high
River tourism	Medium/high
Lake-related tourism	Medium/high
Underwater mineral resources extraction	Medium
Hydro-power	Medium
Maritime fisheries	Low
River fisheries	Low
Lake fisheries	Low
Aquaculture	No consensus opinion among respondents
River transport (including river port development)	No consensus opinion among respondents

Source: Author's elaboration, based on interviews.

Greening traditional blue economy sectors

Green economy initiatives are particularly visible in the shipbuilding sector and mainly consist of introducing new technologies and reducing resource consumption. This is mainly driven by the quantitative benefits of introducing new measures that increase competitiveness by reducing operational costs.

> **Box 3.1. Green measures in the shipbuilding sector – the example of Crist shipyard**
>
> Crist shipyard is a private shipyard company established with the assets of the previous State-owned shipyards. The new owner has switched the company's core activities from simple construction to advanced machinery and building specialised vessels for off-shore sectors. This required investments in advanced technologies and workers skills and resulted in reduced costs (e.g. energy costs).
>
> The limitation of production costs with the use of new technologies brings some environmental advantages. An example of this is metal cutting. Switching from oxy-fuel to plasma sheet metal cutting technology in the Crist shipyard in Gdynia is an example of a green measure which has been applied in Pomorskie. Thanks to the new technology, energy consumption – which contributed substantially to production cost – has been reduced by 60%.
>
> The shipyard's specialised equipment for the offshore sector production was shifted indoors, which allows the gases emitted during the works to be treated via the ventilation systems, rather than being introduced directly into the atmosphere. These actions combine addressing environmental issues with economic benefits, which result in increasing the shipyard's competitiveness.

The implementation of green measures is also evident within the maritime transport sector (see Box 3.2). The interviewed representatives from the logistics and shipbuilding sector highlighted the increasingly common usage of gas-powered (as opposed to mazut-powered) vessels for maritime transportation purposes. The introduction of exceptionally large ships (e.g. Ultra large container ships – ULCS) is also a solution that enables an energy saving per unit of freight transported, which is supported by some studies (Jansson and Shneerson, 1982; Tozer, 2003). However, a more comprehensive set of "greening measures" such as Green Shipping Practices are equally important to take into account when evaluating a firm's "greening" capability in the maritime transport sector (Lun, 2014; Lirn et al., 2014).

Competition from Asian countries in the shipbuilding, transport and logistics sectors forces many Polish shipyards to cut costs. Introducing IT applications is one way of optimising electricity consumption. The market for consulting services on implementing green technologies is developing dynamically and also has the support of EU funding. In the shipbuilding sector, the transition to a greener economy could also mean a switch to other products such as wind turbines. The example of the Harland & Wolff company in the UK (see Box 3.3) shows how companies can build from the skills and expertise of shipbuilding to move towards a more diversified range of products in the renewable energy sector. This is particularly relevant in the Pomorskie region. Potential for implementing green measures also exists in the port sector. One example is the use of dredging spoil from

> **Box 3.2. The Deep Water Terminal in Gdańsk**
>
> The Deep Water Terminal was built in Gdańsk in 2007 to accommodate big container vessels. The concept for the deep water container terminal located in Gdańsk began in the late 90's in order to address the ever growing potential of the Baltic's deep-sea trading routes. DCT Gdańsk was selected by the Port of Gdańsk to design, construct and operate a new independent deep-sea container port that was aimed to be the largest of its kind in the Baltic. The new era for DCT started in May 2011, when the facility started handling the Maersk Line's E-type class container vessels with the capacity of 15.500 TEU, the world's largest ships at that time. Thanks to this milestone, the company joined a prestigious group of North European deep-water container ports, serving the Ultra-Large Container Vessels on the weekly basis, the only such facility East of the Danish Straits (DCT Gdańsk SA, 2015).
>
> As a result of co-operation between regional authorities and private investors, investments have been made in DCT. These investments enabled handling Triple E class container vessels – the biggest in the world. The vessels started to be handled in Gdańsk in 2013. In comparison with older and smaller vessels, the Triple E (Economy of scale, Energy efficient and Environmentally improved) ship production technology is an example of a green measure within the maritime transport sector, as the new ships consume less energy per container. Estimates made during the design phase of the Triple-E have found that the new class could improve CO_2 efficiency by 50% per container compared to the industry average on the Asia-Europe trade lane (Maersk Group, 2015). Electric-powered ships are another example – one such vessel was built by the Northern Shipyard in Gdańsk for a foreign ship owner.
>
> Source: Interviews with representatives of the maritime transport sector.

ports and fairways for building quays. In previous years the spoil was considered a waste and was stored in heaps. Currently, the ports of Gdynia and Gdańsk use it to reinforce quays and build terminals.

In the transport sector, the launch of inland water transport on the Vistula River and its tributaries, for the transportation of bulk goods, was mentioned as a possible way to reduce pollution generated by road transport. The Vistula, the largest river in Poland, could be exploited for freight transport with lower energy consumption than road or rail transport – particularly important in the case of bulk cargo. Nevertheless, the development potential for greening the economy through river transport was perceived as low by many interviewees. This is mainly linked to a perceived deadlock at national level on the issue of the economic exploitation of rivers, with a lack of governmental drivers and an opposition from environmental civil society organisations. In addition, the decision-making process on the exploitation of rivers is perceived as fragmented with seven ministries involved (Ministry of the Environment, Ministry of Agriculture and Rural Development, Ministry of Economy, Ministry of Infrastructure and Development, Ministry of Sport and Tourism, Ministry of Science and Higher Education, Ministry of the Interior).

Regarding tourism, the identified potential for greening the economy relies on several sub-sectors: maritime and coastal tourism, cruises, leisure and recreation, as well as medical services and spas. The potential of river and lake tourism was perceived as lower. Nevertheless, the natural and cultural heritage of the region, combined with its coastal location and a high number of lakes create very favourable conditions for the development

> **Box 3.3. From shipbuilding to wind turbines – the case of Harland & Wolff in the UK**
>
> Harland & Wolff (H&W) is a long-standing heavy engineering company established in 1858 in Belfast. As demand for ocean liners declined with the emergence of the aviation industry and cheaper shipyards around the world reduced their competitiveness, the company diversified into offshore oil and gas markets (constructing offshore platforms, oil rigs, floating production storage and offloading equipment [FPSOs], and drill-ships). In 2002, using the skills and infrastructure from their ship building and offshore platform experience, H&W embarked on a further diversification strategy, changing their name to Harland & Wolff Heavy Industries. While they continue to retain a foothold in the shipbuilding and offshore oil and gas markets, they now also produce a range of renewable energy products, such as turbines for offshore wind farms, wave and tidal energy devices, as well as decommissioning ships at the end of their lives in an environmentally sustainable manner.
>
> The diversification strategy has secured the future of H&W. The company is profitable and stable, despite the difficulties which were apparent at the start of the 2000s. More recently, many heavy engineering companies have struggled because of the global economic downturn. This has had an effect upon Harland and Wolff's traditional markets as well and they have had a number of orders for ships delayed. However the company has remained stable enough to retain a sizeable core staff. The company continues to evolve and has developed expertise in the wind energy sector. It has managed this through transferring skills derived from ship building and manufacturing offshore oil and gas equipment and adapting the workforce and their supply chain to produce wind turbines. In addition, they are at the prototype stage of two wave power generators. The market for such products is at a more immature stage than that of wind power. But by being at the forefront of the technology's development, H&W will be in a strong position to succeed once the product reaches market.
>
> **Adapting the skills in the company and the supply chain**
>
> This more diverse business strategy required expanding the workforce's skills in the company and in the supply chain. Reskilling was required when new equipment was purchased. The training of labourers and fitters was provided and certified by the equipment's manufacturers. The company also has a long-term training programme. This allows for the training of engineers and designers to update their knowledge.
>
> Regarding the skills of the supply chain, the company is collaborating with a trade union. The trade union acts as an employment agency with a pool of temporary workers who can often provide the craft skills required. The agreement with the trade union requires the labour to come from the local area in the first instance. Only if they cannot provide the required skills from the Belfast area, will the trade union provide labour from elsewhere. H&W ensure that the labour provided by the union is of a sufficient quality requesting only workers who have been certified to the required standards (H&W work in a heavily regulated sector, mainly due to the safety implications; a great deal of importance is placed on individuals holding the required certification). On rare occasions, H&W know of a worker in the trade union with a required skill who has not got the relevant certification. When this happens, they will fund a training course for the worker.
>
> For some projects, retraining was not sufficient and the company had to recruit new staff. In such cases, H&W have strong and long-standing links with a number of other engineering companies with greater experience in the renewables sector. They can sub-contract the required skills from these companies for the duration of the project. These relationships are managed through supplier agreements which state the number of workers and level of certification H&W require from their sub-contractors.
>
> *Source:* Miranda, G. et al., 2011.

Box 3.4. Obstacles to greening in the shipbuilding and maritime sector

A perceived lack of vision and overall support for the sector

The national and regional policy frameworks are not sufficiently driving the sector or developing a vision for a green blue economy. Rules on marine resources management that would apply to all concerned parties are not well defined. The decision-making process for maritime policy is fragmented with various ministries involved. Maritime spatial planning is not sufficiently well implemented within the Polish Exclusive Economic Zone although there are numerous planning recommendations produced by VASAB or HELCOM for the Baltic Sea.

There is a lack of consistent strategic vision for the sector with entrepreneurs seeking niches and carrying out contracts relying almost exclusively on their own financial resources. The sector receives limited public support (organisational and financial) especially for promoting innovation and greening practices. Companies are therefore competing with lower labour costs rather than with the development of new technologies. There is limited financial support, such as State subsidies, for energy efficient installations and for limiting emissions from ships. The only way to receive subsidies from the National Environment and Water Fund and the Voivodeship Environment and Water Fund is by upgrading to combined heat and power plants. In addition, there is limited awareness of the benefits of green measures and, in particular, the long-term financial and socio-economic benefits. A detailed calculation of return on investments and potential profit could constitute an incentive to more widely implement green measures.

Limited collaboration with universities and research centres

On the one hand, there is limited awareness within the shipbuilding and maritime sector of the benefits of collaborating with universities and research centres. Companies view scientific research as a high risk as it is unclear whether findings can translate into commercial opportunities. Financial incentives to contribute to research are limited as it is not possible to deduct the cost of research activities from revenues. Universities and research centres are perceived as bureaucratic with lengthy administrative procedures, while scientific researchers are not giving sufficient priority to implementing and commercialising findings.

On the other hand, Polish researchers have limited interest in collaborating with the shipbuilding and maritime sector because of the low-level of wages compared to the remuneration of contributing to international projects. The wages of Polish researchers are several times lower than those of comparably qualified specialists from neighbouring countries such as Sweden, Denmark or Germany.

Shortage of skilled technicians and engineers due to the negative image of jobs within the sector

There is a deficit of workers in the sector, in particular technicians and engineers who would be able to operate the increasingly specialised equipment necessary for the use of new technologies, such as green technologies. In addition, the social image of the sector and the jobs it provides for blue collar workers in shipbuilding, yacht production, logistics and offshore mining industries is not perceived very positively. This makes it difficult to attract future workers and to develop appropriate vocational education for the needs of the maritime sector.

Source: Interviews – shipbuilding and maritime sectors.

of river and lake tourism. The potential for the development of sailing tourism that combines navigating the sea and inland waters is also estimated to be significant. There are plans to develop this branch of tourism, and create new jobs, by exploiting the existing waterways that connect Gdańsk to Żuławy Wiślane, and further – through the Vistula River and existing network of canals – to Berlin. Some local initiatives stimulate innovative forms of recreation, or even entire new sectors of maritime tourism. For example, the Deep Ocean Technology company collaborates with the Technical University of Gdańsk has created an innovative forthcoming business model (see Box 3.6).

> **Box 3.5. Baltic Eco-tourism**
>
> Lessons from the German Baltic coast suggests that "eco-tourism" requires targeting at specific groups. Competition for tourists and the economic benefits they bring to a region is fierce. Schernewski and Sterr (2002) contrast the environmentally attractive island of Usedom on the eastern Baltic coast with the town of Eckernförde on the western Baltic coast, which faces a stagnation of guest numbers. Usedom was experiencing high growth at the time, but environmental quality was regarded as of minor importance for tourism development at the time. High environmental quality was regarded and promoted as the main advantage of Eckernförde, but increasing competition for tourists required the development of a specific image and target group-oriented advertisement. Environmental quality is regarded as one key factor for this.

> **Box 3.6. The Deep Ocean Technology under-water hotel**
>
> The Deep Ocean Technology company began its operations in 2010 in Gdynia. The company is planning the construction of underwater hotels, building manned and remote-controlled underwater vessels, and the construction of seabed penetration installations for low-depth and deep sea purposes. To carry out the technologically complicated tasks, the company initiated collaboration with scientists and engineers at the Faculty of Ocean Engineering and Ship Technology at the Technical University of Gdańsk and other Polish R&D institutions. The company also took advantage of both Polish and foreign shipyards' and equipment producers' manufacturing skills.
>
> Thanks to technological advances, the underwater hotel project *Water Discus* will allow guests not only to dive in the sea but also to stay in luxury underwater accommodation. *Water Discus* constructions will allow guests to inhabit the natural underwater environment of colourful fish, anemones and corals. Hotel guests will also have access to three-person underwater vessels. While the hotel is not operational yet, ongoing work has been undertaken into its technical development.
>
> Source: Deep Ocean Technology, 2014.

Tourism also benefits from green measures to protect natural assets such as marine resources. Although some entrepreneurs highlight that nature preservation measures often limit business opportunities, short-term business needs must be balanced with larger economic and environmental benefits. In the long-term, the protection of marine resources is beneficial, for example due to the potential that a clean environment and highly attractive natural values offer to the development of tourism. The development of green measures in the fisheries sector was perceived as low. Interviewees mentioned that due to EU catch limits on marine fish and rather low possibilities of using rivers and lakes for fish cultivation, maritime, river and lake fisheries have a rather low development potential.

The potential for greening new and emerging sectors

When assessing the new and emerging sectors, renewable maritime energy sources and blue technology were perceived as the sectors with the highest potential for greening the economy in Pomorskie.

Renewable energy sources

The development of wind power in Pomorskie is only in its early stages. The region carried out a study on the "Development Possibilities of the Wind Energy Sector in 2003" (Studium możliwości rozwoju energetyki wiatrowej w województwie pomorskim, 2003). The study concludes that although the Baltic coast enjoys favourable conditions in terms of wind energy resources, the process of locating wind farms encounters numerous obstacles that stem from insufficient information on favouring and limiting factors. Improving the development of wind power stations requires better co-ordination due to possible spatial conflicts surrounding the location of installations and connecting them to the grid via on shore sub-stations and high-voltage and EHV power lines (Spatial Planning Office in Slupsk, 2003).

Nevertheless, the Pomorskie region is experiencing increased in investor interest in wind energy. The proximity of maritime manufacturing and support through the shipbuilding industry is a regional advantage to drive this industry. The Offshore Wind Database notes that between 2011 and 2013 seventy applications were received by the Ministry for Transport, Construction and the Marine Economy totalling approximately 2GW of construction (4 C Offshore, 2015). However, no construction has commenced in the region and the process in still in the planning stage. A transmission network will need to be created to connect the energy produced by offshore power stations to the energy grid on land. This, in turn, will require an analysis of how best to lay cables across the technical and coastal zones and other protected areas. Another problem is that most municipal authorities do not have proactive wind energy policies in place and therefore leave the matter of providing space for wind energy needs to investors and property owners. The introduction of development strategies for wind energy should improve this situation.

According to some respondents, there is also the potential to generate hydropower on the Vistula River. This is not a new idea, as a project for constructing eight high-head dams was developed several decades ago. Today's potential would require the construction of sixteen dams using technology to enable the discharge of accumulated sediments. The construction of the dams could allow the generation of renewable energy, whilst contributing to better aeration of the water, and increasing the population of fish in the river. Raising the water level of the Vistula could increase water retention in the river and also in the catchment areas of its tributaries. This could contribute to improving the management of water resources. Nevertheless, the fragmented decision-making process and the opposition of civil-society groups are undermining the development of such a project. This demonstrates the difficulty of striking a balance between two separate objectives within the green economy: the protection of nature and biodiversity (i.e. the designation of nature protected areas) and the development of renewable energy sources.

Box 3.7. **Obstacles to the blue energy sector**

Lack of coherent policy framework

There is a lack of a coherent vision and policy framework within this sector. The absence of legislation for renewable energy sources means that the energy sector is deprived of systemic support and has been left for an extended period of time in a situation of uncertainty. This is limiting investments in new generation capacities from renewable sources, as well as research on these aspects.

Conflicting interests adding to uncertainties

A number of underlying conflicting interests add to the uncertainties of investing in this sector. For example, small-scale renewable energy entrepreneurs believe that there is not enough support to help connect small-scale electricity producers to the grid. They argue that larger energy companies are lobbying against the creation of new, dispersed renewable energy sources for fear this will decrease their own revenues.

Another example of conflicting interests arises in the hydro-power sector where industries would like to redefine the nature protected areas set up under the European network of nature protected areas "Natura 2000". On the one hand, entrepreneurs believe that the protected areas were delimited arbitrarily in areas without any particular natural values such as ports or post-industrial shorelines. On the other hand, environmental civil society organisations are calling for maximum protection in these areas and for strictly limiting economic activities.

This lack of clarity, along with underlying conflicts over the economic exploitation of rivers, results in limited investments. It also undermines the utilisation of EU support funds for investments into rivers, e.g. from the Connecting Europe Facility.

Environmental concerns perceived as an administrative burden

Measures to protect the environment are often perceived as cumbersome and bureaucratic. Industry representatives mentioned red tape and decision-making inertia, e.g. long waiting periods for decisions on environmental impact assessments. Environmental impact assessments on economic activities and investments are one of the basic instruments for environmental protection in Poland. According to representatives of the hydropower and shipbuilding industries, the costly and lengthy mandatory procedures could be improved and simplified (e.g. global impact assessments in the case of repeated structures on specified, homogenous river stretches, rather than a multiplicity of smaller assessments).

Financial constraints and lack of flexibility for funding programmes

Companies are currently operating under difficult financial constraints and tend to function with short term goals, which make it difficult to plan strategic actions, such as introducing changes in management and organisation to allow the implementation of green measures.

The EU structural programmes do provide funding for investment in the energy sector. However, there is insufficient flexibility to adapt the funding to business needs and to changing market conditions within the framework of the funded project. It is difficult to redirect funding in case technology becomes obsolete or better solutions are identified.

Shortage of skilled workers

There is a shortage of engineers with the technical qualifications required to operate/maintain installations that generate energy from renewable sources, for instance in the hydro-engineering sector.

Source: Interviews with representatives from the energy sector.

Indeed, similar concerns are evident in the generation of wave energy from the Baltic Sea. As a sheltered sea, wave energy is calculated to generate a potential 24 Twh from across coastal areas in Baltic Sea countries, including Poland and the Pomorskie region. Suitable technologies adjusted to local conditions will optimise wave energy production, but there may be impeded by exploitation of the wider blue economy e.g. shipping lanes, fishing zones, marine protected areas, as well as the geo-physical conditions (Heino 2013).

Blue biotechnology

Biotechnology can be defined as "the application of science and technology to living organisms, as well as parts, products and models thereof, to alter living and non-living materials for the production of knowledge, goods and services" (OECD, 2013). Blue biotechnology is the use of marine bio-resources as the target or source of biotechnological applications. The applications of marine biotechnology are wide-ranging: food production, medicine, cosmetics, development of new materials, bioremediation technologies. This suggests the sector has strong potential to address environmental challenges and contribute to greening the economy.

The blue biotechnology sector in the Pomorskie region has considerable prospects for development. Dawidko and Micek (2012) found that intellectual property in the Polish biotechnology sector is spatially concentrated in the biggest metropolitan cities. In this context, Pomorskie's Tri-City is well positioned, together with Warsaw and Kraków, as one of the national leaders in the biotechnology sector. This makes Tri-City an ideal anchor point for the Polish blue biotechnology sector as it is the strongest specialised centre for blue biotechnology in Poland.

The successful future development of the Polish biotechnology sector will depend on its ability to attract talents and researchers. The sector is currently characterised by a large number of small spin-off companies, it requires long period of R&D and presents a high risk of R&D business failure. This is a challenge as specialists are more attracted to larger companies that tend to shape the knowledge networks and are able to attract the most talented specialists. In the forthcoming years, the sector will not generate much employment but it will, however, offer relatively well-remunerated jobs that require high qualifications. Its future will be largely determined by the so-called triple helix – the collaboration of science, public and business sectors. The development of the biotechnology sector in Tri-city is based on collaboration between the Gdańsk Medical University and the University of Gdańsk who created a common Biotechnology Department, and a small number of private companies operating in Pomorksie that are specialised in the field (see Box 3.8).

The University of Gdańsk is currently carrying out research on the Baltic Sea potential for ecosystems services and biotechnology in the Baltic Sea. This may lead to future economic development although the potential of such research is difficult to predict. There are considerable prospects for development within the ecosystem services sector. Ecosystem services are the beneficial outcomes, for the natural environment or people, which result from ecosystem functions (i.e. the physical, chemical, and biological processes or attributes that contribute to the self-maintenance of an ecosystem) (OECD, 2010). These benefits arise from the regulating, supporting, provisioning and cultural services that biodiversity and ecosystems supply. All types of such services, i.e. habitat, provisioning, regulating and cultural services present a high potential for development in Pomorskie.

> **Box 3.8. Public-private partnerships on biotechnology**
>
> The University of Gdańsk and the Gdańsk Medical University have collaborated with a for-profit enterprise to investigate the use of natural marine substances that possess anti-bacterial and anti-cancer qualities. The universities work in partnership with the company Biovico in order to develop and patent their findings. Clinical research carried out by companies in the biotechnology sector has the potential to positively contribute to employment and economic development in the region, while partnerships between the academic sector and the private sector can help to diffuse innovation and establish a regional comparative advantage.
>
> Source: Biovico, 2014.

Some of them are already widely used in sewage and waste treatment. Nonetheless, the scope of their applications remains narrow in comparison to their potential. Extensive research in the field of environmental and natural resources economy (Reyers et al., 2013) is aimed at estimating the economic value of these services and the possibility of including them into the total calculation of economic cost. The regulating ecosystems services such as carbon sequestration and climate regulation, waste decomposition and detoxification, water and air purification, and pest and disease control offer particularly high potential. Opinions varied on the possibilities for underwater resources extraction, hydropower, and aquaculture. These sectors were neither indicated as significant for the economy, nor were they considered irrelevant to the development of Pomorskie. Some argued that seabed oil extraction would be introduced into the region in the future and activities to extract aggregates with high technical parameters and good selection rates would increase.

Aquaculture, thus far undeveloped in Poland, is another area for the potential exploitation of ecosystem services. There is a lack of knowledge on the possibilities of how to exploit the living water resources of the Baltic Sea (especially the bottom invertebrates) for commercial purposes, including consumption. Deficiencies in aquaculture are largely conditioned by the traditional ways of exploiting these resources. The most exploited are fisheries resources (e.g. cod, perch, flounder, plaice, whiting) which have varying levels of sustainable catch. For example the biodiversity indicators developed by the Helsinki Commission for Baltic marine protection, HELCOM (Oesterwind et al., 2013) indicate that the proportion of large fish (principally the dominant stock cod) that live and feed on or near the bottom of seas in the Polish Exclusive Economic Zone (EEZ) has steadily increased over the past decade.

An EEZ is a sea zone prescribed by the United Nations Convention on the Law of the Sea over which a state has special rights. An EEZ reaches from the baseline out to 200 nautical miles (nmi) from its coast (United Nations, 1982). Nevertheless, the stock of other species has slowly recovered, but some have deteriorated. The perspective that fishery resources were depleted was clearly indicated by almost all the interviewed experts and entrepreneurs. So far, the aquaculture of marine invertebrates, especially molluscs, widespread in many EU countries, has not been practiced in the Polish waters of the Baltic Sea. For the past several years many countries in the Baltic Sea region have been witnessing a growing interest in the exploitation of cultivated molluscs – as a highly nutritive food, a means of de-eutrophication of the Baltic Sea, and for removing anthropogenic biomass-related pollution. Additionally, the biomass produced may be exploited in multiple ways within various sectors of the economy, e.g. as farm animal feed or a natural fertiliser (see Box 3.10).

> **Box 3.9. Obstacles to greening in the blue technology and aquaculture sectors**
>
> **Blue technology**
>
> According to specialists, pharmaceutical companies are potentially the strongest and most interested business partners for the development of the blue biotechnology sector. Still, the pharmaceutical companies present within the Polish market fear the risks related to investing in innovative projects. State support in this aspect is limited, while the risk of financial loss is quite high.
>
> Small Polish companies that specialise in the manufacturing of medical substances do not have the financial means for development as expenditures may amount to several million PLN or more. Polish medical regulations on the introduction of new medical substances are similar to those throughout the West. The cost of innovative implementation depends chiefly on the level of necessary testing and procedures. Financially weak, small companies are unable to compete with large, multinational medical corporations. Furthermore, the European patent registration is perceived as a significant financial burden for Polish medical companies, and the renewal fees are often disproportionate to the income they generate. This frequently makes the patenting of inventions economically unviable.
>
> **Inland Fisheries and aquaculture**
>
> Poland has no deep rooted or widespread tradition of exploiting marine resources. Only a small group of fishermen benefit from the economic exploitation of marine, river and lake fauna. One of the interviewees pointed out that "Poles do have a long tradition of farming pigs, not molluscs". The slow weight gain of fish and crustaceans, caused by the low salinity and temperature of the seawater, is the financial and market barrier to the development of aquaculture in the Baltic Sea. These conditions extend the production cycle and therefore reduce any profitability in the sector. Regarding inland fisheries, the short duration of lease contracts (4-5 years) creates a barrier to the better exploitation of Pomorskie's lakes for fish farming purposes. Uncertainty surrounding the extension of contracts makes the full restocking of lakes economically unviable. Meanwhile, the resources could better benefit local economies, and fish processing could generate more jobs.

While marine based aquaculture is virtually non-existent in the Polish EEZ, there is more experience with inland fish production, principally carp and rainbow trout in fish ponds. The FAO reports that in 2005 annual production of carp was 18 000t and rainbow trout 15 700 t with a total estimated value of US $78 million (FAO, 2007). This leads to the question of how Poland can best innovate and expand a sustainable aquaculture industry in its marine estate contributing to a diversified blue economy. Recent outcomes from an EU regional development fund project on Baltic Sea Aquaculture (AQUABEST, 2013) highlights that positive gains could be made from aquaculture in the Baltic Sea region but substantial planning and regulatory reforms are required in addition to social and economic reform.

Multi-sector approaches can reinforce green economy dynamics

Although the transition to a green economy can lead to conflicts over the use of space (for example, conserving marine areas rather than using them for river transport or

> Box 3.10. **Using mussels as a means of waste reduction: Practical Application of the Ecosystem Services concept**
>
> Some of the more interesting findings regarding the exploitation of ecosystem services are the results of the research carried out by the Institute of Oceanography at the University of Gdańsk. The research focused on the use of mussels in the water purification process in the Gulf of Gdańsk. The cultivation of mussels in estuaries or discharge points of water treatment plants, for example, may have a positive impact on water quality, as the mussels store in their tissue the anthropogenic pollution that treatment plants are unable to contain. Based on the data provided by the experimental cultivation of mussels, it has been estimated that per 548 tonnes of nitrogen per year, that are introduced into the Gulf of Gdańsk from the region's largest treatment plant, a 100 hectare cultivation mussels could cut the amount of nitrogen by 36%. The cultivation of mussels may also be used for biological monitoring, i.e. for continuous quality control of the waters in the Gulf of Gdańsk, or as a method of additional purification of the treated sewage from the Gdańsk agglomeration. The cultivated biomass may be used in various ways depending on the type and amount of pollution accumulated. It can serve as a fertiliser for urban greenery, a source of biofuel, or after it is dried, as biomass for heat energy generation. If its quality is sufficient, it may be used in the pharmaceutical industry or cosmetics (e.g. for obtaining collagen) or as a component of animal feed. Another important aspect of introducing the cultivation of mussels and other marine organisms is the activation of local communities, through the creation of new jobs in the aquaculture sector – a sector of the maritime economy that has not yet been developed in Poland.
>
> So far, research on the experimental cultivation of mussels in the Gulf of Gdańsk has concluded positively. The next step would be to progress from experimental to semi-industrial cultivation. However, a lack of funding means that any further actions, and their eventual exploitation on a larger scale, are unlikely to take place.
>
> *Source:* University of Gdańsk, 2014.

hydropower), greening measures in one sector can also have beneficial impacts for others. In 1992, the Hel Marine Station of the University of Gdańsk began its operations on the Hel Peninsula. They included, among others, the protection of the grey seal and the harbour porpoise in the southern Baltic Sea (see Box 3.11). Following its initial stages of being a strictly scientific facility, the seal centre (*fokarium*) that operates as a part of the Marine Station has become an important education and tourism centre, both on a national and international scale. Scientific and educational activities, the promotion of the natural marine environment, and the subsequent development of educational tourism have led to the establishment of new restaurants and accommodation services, which in turn increases government income, investment and job creation.

Another example of a multi-sector approach is the construction of wind power stations in Pomorskie alongside the need to monitor birds, which may be exposed to the negative effects of the power stations' functions. Technological progress allows the implementation of green measures in this case. Information on bird migration is now collected automatically, excluding the need for workers to visit the power stations. Hence, the long-term cost of monitoring is being reduced, as well as the pollution generated by the means of transport that would have been used by the workers to reach the power stations for data collection purposes.

> **Box 3.11. Initiative for the protection of marine resources in the Baltic Sea**
>
> The Hel Marine Station of the Institute of Oceanography at the University of Gdańsk began its activities in 1992. The creation of the Hel Marine Station came as a result of research into the anthropogenic degradation of the natural environment of the Gulf of Gdańsk, the Bay of Puck and the coastal sea regions. The Hel Marine Station is particularly well placed for research on the functioning and the protection of life forms in the Baltic Sea. It operates within a framework of multilateral study contracts on the international, as well as national, level.
>
> In 1999, the *fokarium* was created as a part of this scientific and educational facility for the reintroduction and protection of the grey seal in the southern Baltic Sea Region. The main objective was the creation of a centre to support the protection of and dissemination of information on the species. Through its biological, veterinary and breeding studies on seals, the centre contributes in a practical way to international action for the protection of this species in the Baltic Sea Region. The centre releases recovered seals, and young seals born in captivity back into their natural environment. Releasing the seals serves to balance the losses sustained by the Baltic population as a result of irresponsible human activity (sea pollution, fisheries and other interference). The aim of releasing the animals is to allow them to play the positive role of predator in the Baltic Sea and to test the cleanliness of the marine ecosystem, e.g. the quality of the fish that humans eat.
>
> The Hel Marine Station runs the Blue School project (Błękitna Szkoła), which is aimed at elementary and secondary school students. It offers classes and courses, including field activities, dedicated to marine and coastal ecology. The highly ergonomic layout of the seal centre allows for free observation of the seal breeding process, while the education and promotion initiatives of the Hel Marine Station make it a major national and international tourist attraction, thus increasing the touristic values of Hel and extending the season to cover almost the entire year.
>
> *Source:* University of Gdańsk, 2014.

> **Box 3.12. Resolving Conflicting Objectives: The Scottish National Marine Plan (NMP)**
>
> The National Marine Plan sits at the heart of planning for the future of Scotland Seas. The plan is undergoing final examination (as of March 2015) by the Scottish Parliament and set policies for the sustainable development of Scotland's seas out to 200nm with a vision for clean, healthy, safe, productive and biologically diverse oceans and seas. The legislative driver for the NMP is the Marine (Scotland) Act 2010 and establishes that that marine plans set economic, social and marine ecosystem objectives and objectives relating to the mitigation of, and adaptation to, climate change. The NMP brings together a number of strategic objectives for renewable energy, fisheries, aquaculture marine protection, recreation, ports and a number of relevant maritime sectors. The objectives are guided by the ecosystem approach and are designed to meet the criteria for Good Environmental Status under the EU Marine Strategy Framework Directive. Public authorities across government must take their decisions in accordance with the objectives in the plan.
>
> The NMP explicitly addresses potential conflicts between maritime sectors and seeks to maximise co-locational opportunities including the identification of regions for wind, wave and tidal development. Under the NMP a series of regional planning regimes will be developed that take a local focus and be delivered by Marine Planning Partnerships. Regional plans will be in accordance with the NMP and guide local development.

Conclusions

There is strong potential for both traditional and newly emerging blue economy sectors to lead the green economy transition in the Pomorskie region. Pomorskie is an attractive Polish region with traditionally strong blue economy sectors such as fisheries, tourism, maritime transport and shipbuilding. In sectors such as shipbuilding, the need to remain competitive at international level and finding new niche markets are major drivers for lowering operational costs such as energy bills and establishing greener practices. The sectors also need to evolve to offer a wider range of products. In this context, investments in the green economy are important to facilitate the structural transition. The recent closure of two major production shipyards, Gdynia and Szczecin, has had a massive social cost, with the closure of the Gdynia shipyard alone estimated at having doubled unemployment in the area. The two shipyards provided almost 12 000 jobs in 2007 and were among the region's largest employers. Understanding how best to utilise the skills of the now "redundant" shipbuilders is extremely important.

In other sectors, the benefits stemming from a greener economy are more indirect. For instance, the tourism industry and recreational activities sectors will benefit from nature preservation and water quality. New sectors are emerging, such as the blue biotechnology sector, with a strong potential for promoting the green economy. Nevertheless, a number of obstacles are undermining developments, such as the fragmented policy framework and decision-making process, conflicting interests over the use of space, lack of financing opportunities, and skills shortages, in particular for technicians.

Notes

1. Pre-productive age group: population 17 years or less, productive age group: 18-59 years for women and 18-64 for men, post-productive age: 60 or more years for women and 65 or more for men.

References

4 C Offshore (2015), *Global Offshore Wind Farms Database*, (Online) *www.4coffshore.com/windfarms/* (accessed 8 June 2017).

AQUABEST (2013), *AQUABEST Recommendations: Developing responsible aquaculture in the Baltic Sea Region*.

Biovico (2014), *Nutraceutyki – Biovico*, (online) *http://biovico.pl/en/* (accessed 8 June 2017).

Biuro Planowania Przestrzennego w Słupsku [Spatial Planning Office in Słupsk] (2003), *Studium możliwości rozwoju energetyki wiatrowej w województwie pomorskim* [The Study of Development Possibilities of Wind Energy Sector in Pomorskie Voivodeship], Słupsk.

Dawidko, P. and G. Micek (2012), "Labour flows in the biotech sector in Poland", *Prace Geograficzne*, 130, Instytut Geografii i Gospodarki Przestrzennej, Uniwersytet Jagieloński, pp. 73-89.

Deep Ocean Technology (DOT) (2014), *Underwater Hotel*, *www.deep-ocean-technology.com/pl* (accessed 16 November 2014).

DCT Gdańsk SA, (2015), *Deepwater Container Terminal Gdańsk*, (online) *www.portgdansk.pl/about-port/dct-gdansk* (accessed 2017 June 8].

European Commission (2012), "COM (2012) 494 Communication from the Commission to the European Parliament, the European Economic and Social Committee and the Committee of the Regions",*Blue Growth – opportunities for marine and maritime sustainable growth*, *http://ec.europa.eu/maritimeaffairs/policy/blue_growth/documents/com_2012_494_en.pdf*.

FAO (2007), *Fishery Country Profile: Poland*, *www.fao.org/fi/oldsite/FCP/en/Pol/profile.htm*, (accessed 9 June 2017).

Główny Urząd Statystyczny (GUS) [Central statistical office] (2014), *Portal Informacyjny*, *www.stat.gov.pl* (accessed 16 September 2014).

Heino, H. (2013), *Utilisation of Wave Power in the Baltic Sea Region*, Finland Futures Research Centre, University of Turku, ISBN 978-952-249-272-2.

Instytutu Badań nad Gospodarką Rynkową [Institute for Market Economics] (2008), *Identyfikacja potencjalnych klastrów na bazie analizy struktury gospodarki województwa pomorskiego* [Identification of potential clusters based on analysis of the structure of the economy Pomorskie voivodship], Gdańsk.

Invest in Pomerania (2014), *Invest in Pomerania*, www.investinpomerania.pl (accessed 28 October 2014).

Jansson, J. and D. Shneerson (1982), "The optimal size ship", *Journal of Transport Economics and Policy*, 16(3), pp. 217-238.

Lirn, T.C., H. Lin and K.C. Shang (2014), "Green shipping management capability and firm performance in the container shipping industry", *Maritime Policy & Management: The flagship journal of international shipping and port research*, 41:2, pp. 159-175, http://dx.doi.org/10.1080/03088839.2013.819132.

Lun, V.L. (2014), "Development of green shipping network to enhance environmental and economic performance", *Polish Maritime Research*, Vol. 20, Issue Special Issue, pp. 13-19, ISSN (Print) 1233-2585, http://dx.doi.org/10.2478/pomr-2013-0023.

Maersk Group (2015), *Sustainability Report 2015*, Cophenhagen: A.P. Moller – Maersk Group.

Miranda, G. et al. (2011), "Climate Change, Employment and Local Development in Poland", *OECD Local Economic and Employment Development (LEED) Working Papers*, No. 2011/22, OECD Publishing, Paris, http://dx.doi.org/10.1787/5kg0nvfvwjd0-en.

Nietupski, S. (2010), *Raport dot.yczący Przemysłu Jachtowego w Polsce, Polska Izba Przemysłu Jachtowego i Sportów Wodnych – POLBOAT* [Report on the Yachting Industry in Poland, the Polish Chamber of Marine Industry and Water Sports], Warsaw.

OECD (2013), *Marine Biotechnology: Enabling Solutions for Ocean Productivity and Sustainability*, OECD Publishing, Paris, http://dx.doi.org/10.1787/9789264194243-en.

OECD (2010), *Paying for Biodiversity: Enhancing the Cost-Effectiveness of Payments for Ecosystem Services*, OECD Publishing, Paris, http://dx.doi.org/10.1787/9789264090279-en.

Oesterwind, D. et al. (2013), "HELCOM corei of biodiversity proportion of large fish in the community", *Core Indicator Report* (accessed March 2015).

Reyers, B., R. Biggs, G.S. Cumming, T. Elmqvist, A.P. Hejnowicz and S. Polasky (2013), "Getting the measure of ecosystem services: a social-ecological approach", *Frontiers in Ecology and the Environment*, 11: 268-273, http://dx.doi.org/10.1890/120144.

Sagan, I., C. Martinez-Fernandez and T. Weyman (2013), "Pomorskie Region: Responding to Demographic Transitions Towards 2035", *OECD Local Economic and Employment Development (LEED) Working Papers*, No. 2013/07, OECD Publishing, Paris, http://dx.doi.org/10.1787/5k48189zpsmw-en.

Schernewski, G. and H. Sterr (2001), "Tourism and environmental quality of the German Baltic Coast: Conflict or chance?", Schernewski, G. and U. Schiewer (eds), *Baltic Coastal Ecosystems: Structure, Function and Management*, Ceedes-Series, Springer, Berlin, pp. 215-229.

Stacja Morska Instytutu Oceanografii Uniwersytetu Gdańskiego [Institute of Oceanography at the University of Gdańsk] (2014), www.hel.ug.edu.pl/ (accessed 16 November 2014).

Tarkowski, M. (2013), "Sytuacja gospodarcza województwa pomorskiego w II kwartale 2013 r" [The economic situation in the Pomeranian province in the second quarter of 2013], in *Pomorski Przegląd Gospodarczy* [Pomeranian Economic Review], www.ppg.ibngr.pl, (accessed 11 October 2014).

Tozer, D. (2003), "Ultra-large container ships: The green ships of the future?", *Lloyd's Register*, London.

United Nations (1982), *United Nations Convention on the Law of the Sea – Part V*, (online) www.un.org/depts/los/convention_agreements/texts/unclos/part5.htm (accessed 8 June 2017).

University of Gdańsk (2014), *Hel Marine Station*, (online) http://arch.en.ug.edu.pl/?&id_art=132&lang=en (accessed 8 June 2017).

Further reading

Actia Forum Sp. z o.o. (2009), *Studium rozwoju strategicznego małych portów i przystani morskich w województwie pomorskim* [Study of strategic development of small ports and harbours in Pomorskie], Gdynia.

Granatowicz, J., W. Majewski and R. Szymkiewicz (2013), *Kaskada Dolnej Wisły szansą dla Polski – opracowanie autorskie, maszynopis.*

Protasiuk, A. et al. (2014), "Założenia Programu Wisła", *Ekologia, Przyszłoś?, Równowaga – streszczenie menadżerskie,* [Assumptions of the Vistula Program, Ecology, Future, balance – a summary of management], Gdańsk.

VASAB (2010), *VASAB Long-Term Perspective for the Territorial Development of the Baltic Sea Region,* Riga.

Chapter 4

Greening company practices and the impact on skills in the blue economy sectors

This chapter presents the results of an OECD company survey with businesses in Pomorskie to understand the extent to which local companies are "greening" their workplace practices, products and services. The majority of firms surveyed are small and medium sized (SMEs) enterprises with business operations focused primarily in the Pomorskie region. The survey results indicate that companies face a number of real and perceived barriers to adopting green practices. Many are turning to business associations as training partners as opposed to universities or vocational education institutions. This survey also provides insights as to which skills are needed to boost the blue economy in Pomorskie.

Blue economy sectors have a strong potential for leading the transition to a green economy in Pomorskie. However, are individual businesses leveraging on these opportunities today? How do companies perceive the transition to a green economy? What is the impact on skills and jobs? To respond to these questions, a survey of businesses in Pomorskie was carried out during the autumn of 2014. Company surveys were carried out to identify the extent to which businesses are greening their practices, products and services and the related impact on skills and jobs. Companies also assessed the responsiveness of the local skills ecosystems and the level of knowledge sharing activities within networks and clusters. Survey results were complemented by interviews with selected firms and stakeholders, particularly 26 bilateral interviews with businesses, training providers and regional authorities.

The survey was conducted to get an indication of how firms are positioning themselves in the green transition. Almost 3 000 companies were contacted by phone (out of an estimated sample of 6 400 companies operating in the selected sectors during September and October 2014). 124 companies completed the survey. The majority of the firms surveyed were small and medium sized enterprises, namely. Figure 4.1 specifies that nearly half of the firms surveyed employ less than ten people.

Figure 4.1. **Size of the surveyed companies**

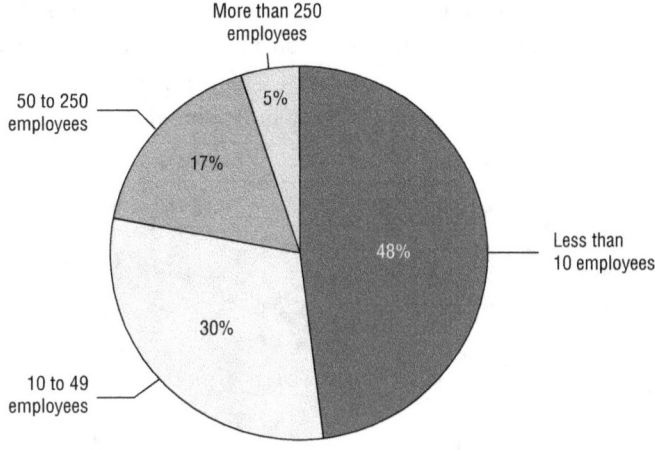

Source: OECD, 2014.

The majority of the responding firms operate mainly at the local (40%) or regional level (16%) as opposed to the national (24%) or international level (25%). While the representatives of medium and large enterprises defined the range of their operations as national or international, the micro and small enterprises tended to focus on the local and regional markets. The low number of responses in some selected sectors does not always allow sector comparisons.

Figure 4.2. **Main economic sectors of the surveyed companies**

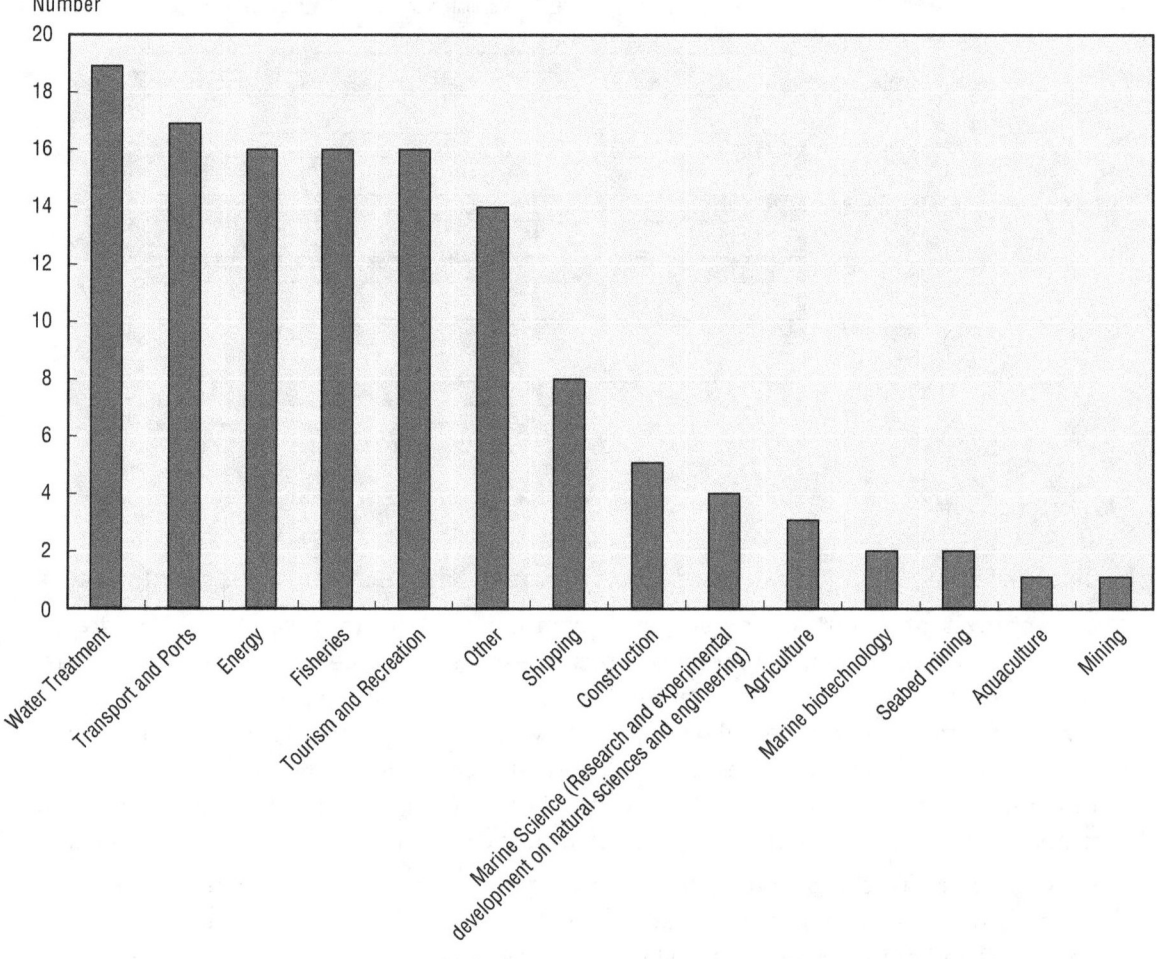

Source: OECD, 2014.

Most firms in Pomorskie consider environmental issues to pose minor challenges to their businesses

The survey started by reviewing companies' perceptions of the environmental challenges. Overall, the majority of businesses consider **environmental challenges** as **minor challenges**. For example, close to 70% of respondents considered the protection of biodiversity and air quality minor challenges. The most prominent challenge for businesses in Pomorskie is **energy consumption**. Close to 50% of the businesses surveyed consider this a strong or moderate challenge. **Raw material efficiency** and **waste management** were also viewed as relatively more challenging than other issues. In general, the challenges that entrepreneurs perceive as strong are more closely linked to operating costs or to regulatory compliance (mandatory waste segregation, gas emissions standards). There are no significant differences between responses received by sector. However, there are variations in responses depending on company size. Micro-enterprises (less than 3 employees) tend to consider environmental challenges as minor, while larger companies are more inclined to report stronger challenges associated with environmental issues.

Figure 4.3. **Identified environmental challenges**

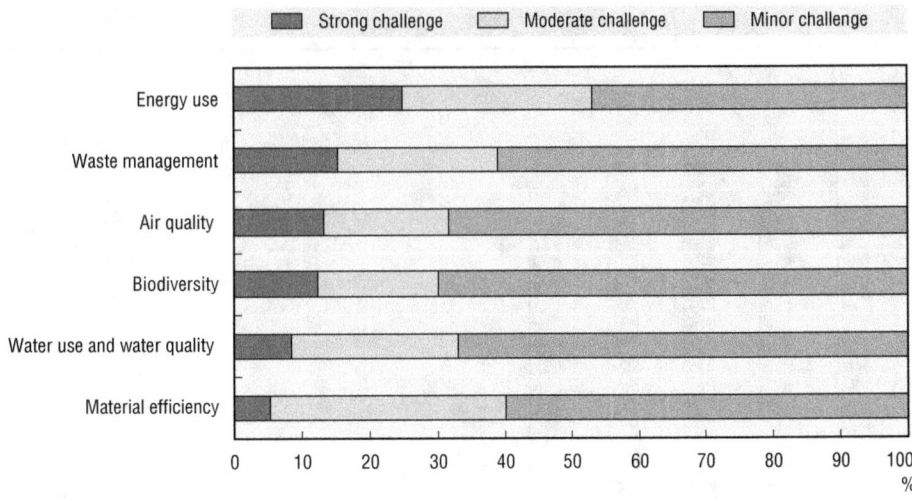

Source: OECD, 2014.

Most companies have introduced green measures in their business practices

Approximately 60% of the surveyed companies claim to have introduced green measures in their business practices. Green measures were described very broadly as measures related to processes or products, implemented with a positive impact on the environment and environmental protection. However, this does not necessarily mean that business practices have been reshaped to integrate sustainability. 63% of companies who implemented green measures introduced only a limited number of them. Only 3% of companies that have implemented green measures claim to have reshaped their business.

Companies were also required to assess what these green measures related to. Pollution reduction was the green measure most frequently mentioned, which would tend to confirm that regulatory compliance (emission standards) plays an important role. Nature conservation also ranks highly, which somewhat contradicts the fact that most of the surveyed firms view biodiversity as a minor challenge. Again, no major differences were observed by sector, but company size did seem to have an influence on responses. Larger companies (more than 250 employees) tend to have introduced more green measures than smaller businesses.

Regulatory compliance remains the main driver for greening business practices

There is a wide range of reasons for companies to introduce green measures in their business activities. These may be economic or non-economic, e.g. formal and legal, socio-cultural or related to brand image. Among the surveyed companies in Pomorskie, complying with regulations is indicated as the most prominent driver for introducing green measures in business activities. Benefits to brand image, company values, and savings on operational costs also rank high on the list of drivers. The survey revealed that pressure from NGOs, local governance institutions, labour unions and managerial vision had more limited impact.

The survey results show different motivations depending on the size of the company. In larger companies, company values and code of conduct, as well as brand image, are more frequently mentioned as a significant driver for implementing green measures. In smaller companies, reducing operational costs is more frequently mentioned as a key driver. Regulation compliance turned out to be a significant motivator primarily for medium and large companies.

> **Box 4.1. Approaches to environmental regulation by industries and regions**
>
> Sustainable development and the regulation of environmental issues is a relatively recent policy direction for the EU, but the EU strategy for "smart, sustainable and inclusive growth" clearly suggests that it is growing in importance and scope (European Commission, 2010). At the firm level, environmental legislation – as part of sustainable development – often equates compliance with environmental legislation as raising costs. Some suggest that this need not be the case, arguing that environmental regulation induces innovation by raising industry's awareness of otherwise missed opportunities. Whether regulation, and the need to improve environmental performance, is viewed as an economic opportunity to innovate or as a threat that must be complied with can be attributed in part to company "mind-set" (Porter and van der Linde, 1995).
>
> Evidence from the European steel industry, as well as from the decline of coal industry in the Ruhr and South Wales Valleys regions, points to the importance of institutional configurations for shaping firm and regional approaches to innovating on "green" transitions. Such configurations are important for regions, too, in the way environmental regulation might be viewed as a "beneficial constraint". The longer-term orientation evident in Germany, for example, has facilitated the creation of a framework of environmental regulation, long-term protection and sustainability, with climate change mitigation enshrined in legislation. This framework has stimulated green economic activity in the Ruhr regeneration, as well as innovative approaches within highly polluting sectors/firms. The outcome is a *developmental* perspective, credited with encouraging investments in human capital and low-carbon technology, leading to an impressive record on export orientated innovation, particularly within engineering and manufacturing sectors (Stroud et al., 2015; Stroud and Evans, 2014).
>
> In the UK, short-term financial perspectives dominate firm perspectives, with a focus on *compliance* with environmental regulation rather than innovation. Where innovation is a focus, it is on immediate cost reduction rather than on longer-term strategies (involving, for example, workforce development). More broadly, the necessary infrastructures – as well as social and political support – are not configured to facilitate a capital-intensive, high-skill trajectory in transitioning toward a green economy. For example, two flagship Welsh Government initiatives are aimed at construction/building retrofit, and thus are representative of a low-carbon technology *implementation activity*. The focus is on installation, implying import of higher value-added and skilled inputs, with little scope for generating substantial export revenues (Stroud et al., 2015; Stroud and Evans, 2014).

Financial and administrative barriers are the most frequently mentioned obstacles to greening practices

Companies may face various legal, social or financial obstacles to greening their practices. The most significant perceived barrier was financial, with high costs or lack of funding for implementing green measures. There was wide variation in the responses from businesses depending on sector and company size. More than 70% of the companies interviewed mentioned financial barriers in the energy (93%), construction (83%), water treatment (73%) and fisheries (70%) sectors. A majority of companies (around 60%) considered financial barriers an issue in the shipbuilding and maritime (transport and port) sector.

Figure 4.4. **Main drivers of greening measures in companies**

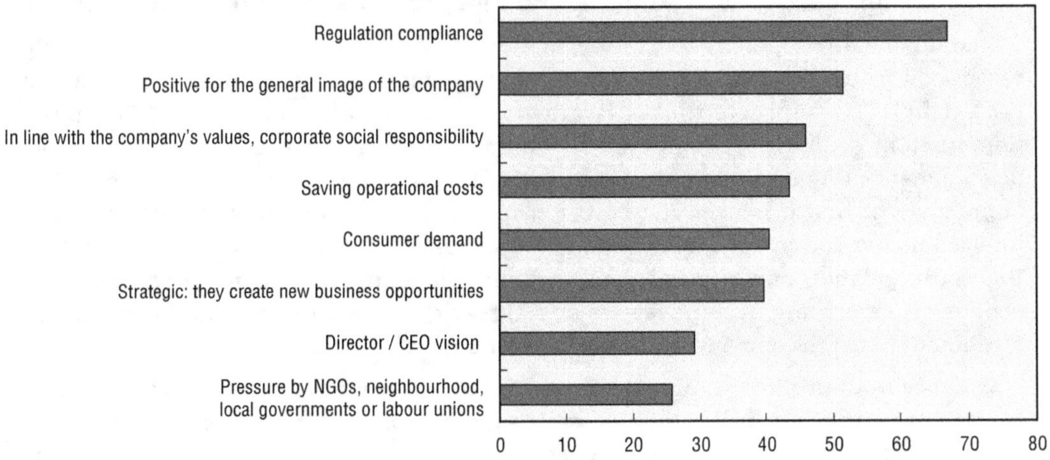

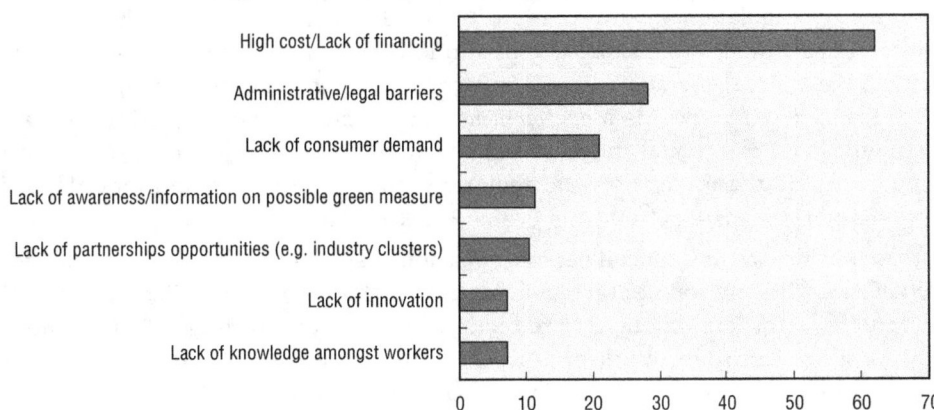

Source: OECD, 2014.

Figure 4.5. **Obstacles to green measures**

Source: OECD, 2014.

However, financial barriers were mentioned by only 37% of companies in the tourism and recreation sector, and 16.7% in the marine science and biotechnology sector. Similarly, financial barriers are mainly perceived as an obstacle to implementing green measures in businesses of between 10 and 49 employees (81% of companies of this size consider financing an issue). In contrast, only 50% of micro-companies (3 or less employees) mention financing as a major barrier. Companies also perceive legal and administrative barriers as a significant obstacle to greening their practices. This is also evident from the interview results which portray green practices as a cumbersome administrative process. The skills and knowledge of workers and the promotion of innovation are not perceived as major obstacles.

The impact of greening on skills and jobs in the marine economy sectors: need for technical skills

While companies do not frequently mention skills shortages and gaps as a major obstacle to greening their practices, 65% of Pomorskie's companies that have implemented green measures in their business practices had to address the issue of skills. They did so by hiring consultancy services (40%), by up-skilling or retraining current staff (40%) or by hiring new staff (20%). Often, they combined these various ways of addressing skills (e.g. consultancy services were combined with the retraining of current employees). Interestingly, hiring new staff for greening business practices is the least frequent option for dealing with the transition to a greener economy. This highlights that implementing a green transition does not translate systematically into job creation, but does still raise the question of training workers and providing adequate skills. According to the survey, the occupations most frequently required for the greening of the blue economy sectors are the professional and technical occupations (more than 60%) as well as skilled tradespersons and machine operators (30%). The level of requirement for administrative, legal and clerical occupations (15%) is also quite high.

Figure 4.6. **Obstacles to green measures**

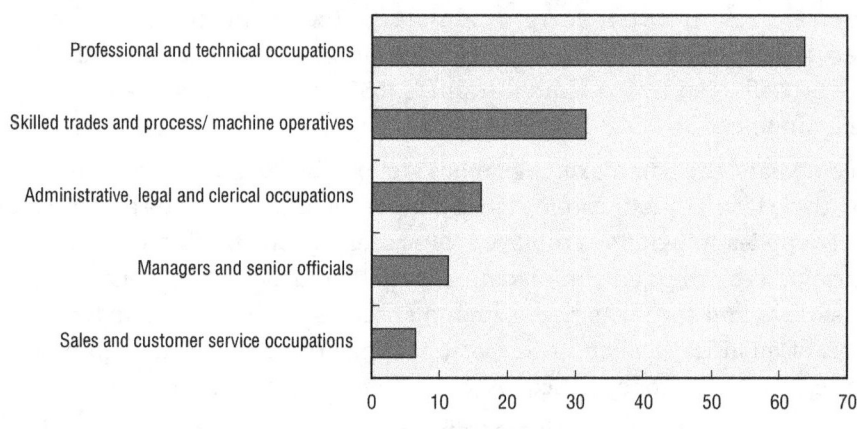

Source: OECD, 2014.

Regarding the type of skills required for the transition to a green economy, companies emphasised the need for advanced technical skills, such as legal skills and skills in scientific research (over 50%). Interpersonal and entrepreneurial skills were also rather frequently mentioned in the company survey. Management and IT skills, as well as foreign language were, according to the companies' representatives, less relevant for the implementation of green measures.

Figure 4.7. **Most frequently required skills for implementation of green measures**

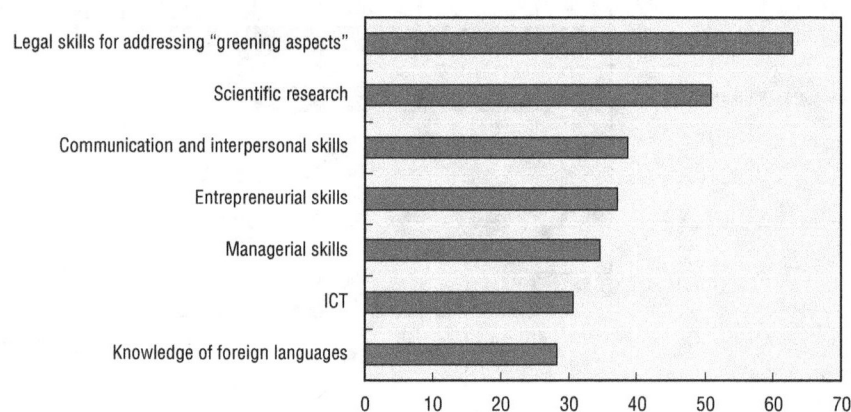

Source: OECD, 2014.

The survey results therefore draw special attention to technical skills. This was confirmed by the interviews with stakeholders undertaken as part of the fieldwork for this OECD study. For instance, interviewees pointed to the importance of designing skills, as well as the ability to interpret technical drawings and to operate specialised equipment. Multi-language skills proved to be highly valued in the logistics and maritime transport sectors (Provincial Labour Office in Gdańsk, 2013) although the survey does not identify them as the most relevant skills needed.

The skills ecosystems: training providers and obstacles to training

Of the companies that offered their employees training on the implementation of green measures (around 25% of total companies), over 70% offered on-the-job training, during working hours, while slightly more than 60% offered off-the-job training – either on company premises or outside. Approximately 10% of the companies offered their employees both options. The majority of companies thought it was important for the training to be delivered by accredited trainers (65%) and to provide a formal (nationally recognised) qualification (75%).

In recent years, the Pomorskie region has stepped up its effort to validate *informal skills*. Workers with no formal qualifications are gaining recognition (Miranda and Larcombe, 2012). This usually applies to persons employed in or seeking jobs that do not require advanced competencies. Certified qualifications are especially crucial in the logistics and maritime transport sectors and for posts that demand specialised technical competencies. Formal certification of qualifications on lower positions may be obtained through participation in courses (often obligatory for specific jobs) carried out by accredited trainers.

Training was carried out by private training companies and other institutions, such as business associations, technical institutes, chambers of industry and labour unions. The most common opinion among the entrepreneurs of the Pomorskie Voivodeship was that the best partners for the implementation of green measures were the professional associations (around 45% of all answers) and the private training companies (around 35% of answers). Slightly less frequently, the entrepreneurs pointed to technological institutes and universities, as providers of training on green measures.

Figure 4.8. **Skills ecosystems training providers**

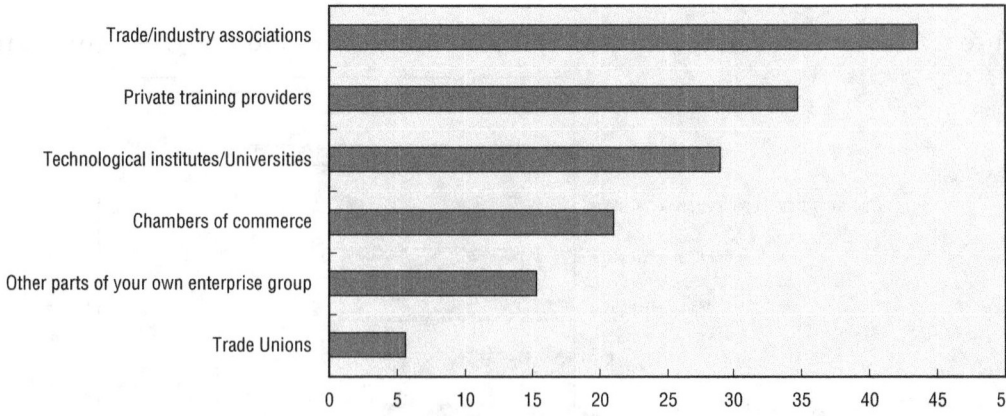

Source: OECD, 2014.

Research conducted by M. Kubisz (2011) shows that training companies were considered to be the most important entities in the local "ecosystem" of learning. At the same time, business organisations, NGOs and higher education centres were deemed to be the least relevant elements of this "ecosystem". These results also applied to the non-formal methods of gaining power. In comparison to the results of same research conducted in the region of Zagłębie, i.e. a region of Poland with low saturation of business environment institutions, Pomorskie stands out in terms of high position of professional associations.

How reactive is the training system to companies' needs?

Companies in Pomorskie have a rather positive view on the flexibility and reactivity of the training system to deliver their training needs. 75% of the companies were confident that it would take less than 6 months for relevant training to be organised to cover their training needs (55% believed it would take less than 3 months). Nevertheless, the survey highlighted a number of shortcomings and obstacles. Overall, companies consider that cost is the most significant obstacle to providing training on green business practices (70% of the surveyed companies). Other important obstacles include the availability of training in the region and the lack of information on existing training opportunities (35% of the surveyed companies). Finally, 30% of companies also pointed to the timing of training as an obstacle. The importance of such obstacles tends to vary between sectors. In the energy sector and the water treatment sector, the most prominent obstacles were the cost of training and the availability of training in the region. In the traditional blue economy sectors (mining and seabed mining, fisheries and aquaculture, transport and port, shipbuilding, tourism and recreation), the cost of training and the lack of information on available training opportunities were identified as the main obstacles.

Figure 4.9. **Obstacles to training**

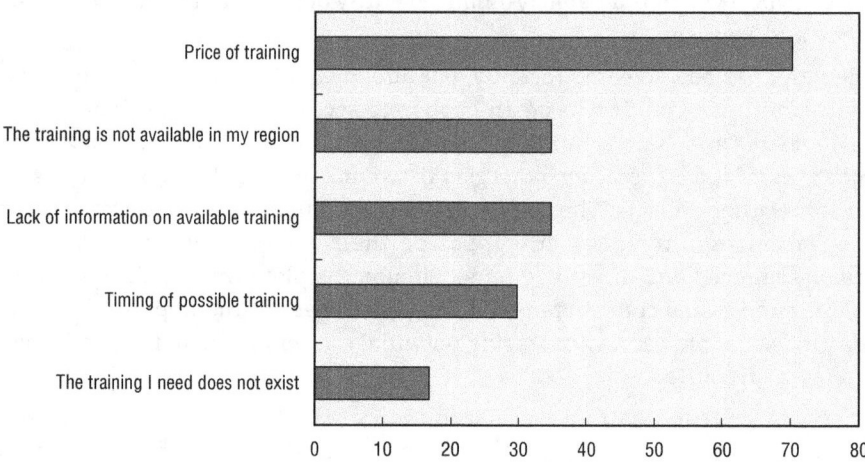

Source: OECD, 2014.

Knowledge sharing activities remain limited

Knowledge, common contacts and information flow are vital elements of policy implementation that increase policy effectiveness. There is limited collaboration between entrepreneurs and regional public authorities, professional organisations and universities, in order to increase knowledge on the developments and innovation in the sector of their economic activities. Networks of this nature can help disseminate best practices and mobilise investments in green economy projects as in the example of the green entrepreneurship network in Spain. Less than one in five entrepreneurs claims to collaborate within a business cluster or industry association to keep abreast of developments and innovation in their sector. Collaboration with university, local government or foreign partners is negligible (less than 5%). The preferred sources of information for businesses include specialised magazines and websites.

> Box 4.2. **The Green Entrepreneurship Network in Spain**
>
> The Red Emprendeverde (Green Entrepreneurship Network) is a platform created to support business creation in green sectors or green-related activities. This network was created by the Fundación Biodiversidad (Biodiversity Foundation), a public foundation of the Spanish Government, related to the National Ministry of Environment and Rural and Marine Development. The Foundation aims at preserving the natural heritage and the biodiversity while creating employment, wealth and well-being in the society. The Foundation collaborates with entities and institutions in the public sector, the civil society and business environment.
>
> The Green Entrepreneurship Network seeks to Foster Entrepreneurship and business growth in sectors or activities related to the environment protection. The Network provides support to entrepreneurs and business owners through 1) the draft or redefinition of the business plan, 2) bringing investors and entrepreneurs together, and 3) the provision of training and technical assistance. The Network also organises contests to encourage quality projects while supporting financially some of the most promising initiatives.
>
> Members of the Network include entrepreneurs, investors, or any other actor interested in seizing the economic opportunities arising from the green economy. The Network is co-financed by European Social Fund (ESF). The Network benefits of the collaboration of the Spanish Network of Business angels, the Triodos Bank, and the National Innovation Enterprise (ENISA) which is a publicly-financed entity of the National Ministry of Industry, Commerce and Tourism.
>
> The network has been created recently, but already made an important contribution to launching enterprise creation in green economic sectors. The Network brings together over 400 investors and various hundreds of potential entrepreneurs. It has also stimulated the exchanges of ideas, creating synergies between some of the ideas and also adding value to some other projects. The contest has also permitted the identification of some of the most promising projects, and supported their development indirectly (courses, technical assistance,) and directly (grants). Finally, the platform and the communication around this project has contributed to raising awareness of the opportunities emerging from the green economy and encouraging potential entrepreneurs to further develop their idea in a more structured way.
>
> The network contributed to a clear definition of the terms: green enterprise, green entrepreneur, eco-investor and other stakeholders in the green activities. The on-line platform (www.redemprendeverde.es) facilitates the dissemination of best practices to a wider market. The platform also brings investors (venture capitalists, business angels, banks) closer to the ideas (entrepreneurs, businesses) so that it makes it easier for them to meet and make businesses in a sector of common interest. The platform serves as social network for entrepreneurs, investors and other actors to exchange and consolidate ideas. It also centralises the services offered by the network (monitoring, technical assistance, training courses) in a one-stop-shop, easy to access.
>
> *Source:* Miranda et al., 2011.

Support needed from the public sector

Collaboration within the framework of regional policy may take different forms, for example aiding entrepreneurs to take adequate actions. The survey results reveal that, in terms of the green growth of the region, the most desired form of aid from public authorities is investment support for purchasing machines and equipment, as well as financial incentives that support the employment of new workers (over 40% of respondents declared that such assistance was indispensable). It is the micro-companies that expect this form of support, since as single entities they may fear large investments.

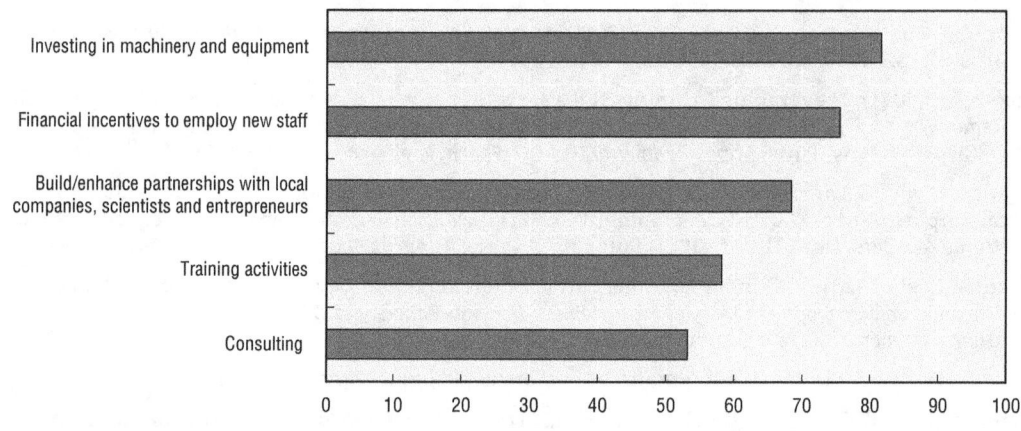

Figure 4.10. **Activities requiring public sector support**

Source: OECD, 2014.

According to the respondents, fostering partnerships between local entrepreneurs and scientists is not as crucial. A significant proportion of entrepreneurs (over 20%), declared that they did not expect any support in the form of training and consultation on technological processes, potential assessment, competition analysis or market trends, for example. The importance placed on fostering consultations and partnerships was similar regardless of company size (the representatives of small, medium and large companies displayed a similar approach to the issue). In light of these facts, the regional public sector should undertake actions to raise the awareness and the motivation of entrepreneurs to increase their knowledge on green measures, and should prepare an appropriate training offer to attract companies. Both the public and private sectors play an equally important role in the implementation of green measures in activities related to water resources management.

Conclusions

Transitioning to a greener economy is not a priority for companies in the blue economy and water sectors in Pomorskie. Companies tend to consider environmental challenges as minor challenges. They do not view greening as an opportunity, but rather as a cumbersome financial and administrative process, and greening measures are mainly driven by compliance with regulations. Although a majority of companies (61%) claim to have implemented green measures, very few companies (5%) have become green champions and reshaped their businesses completely.

While companies do not frequently mention skills shortages and gaps as a major obstacle to greening their practices, 65% of Pomorskie's companies that have implemented green measures in their business practices had to address the issue of skills. Training current employees and using external consultancy services are two of the firms' strategies to address skills gaps in their transition towards greener practices. The responsiveness of the training system is perceived as good, as training can quickly be adapted to companies' needs. However, for the major blue economy sectors, there is still a lack of information on training opportunities. The cost of training is also an obstacle. The majority of firms would turn to their business associations as a major training partner. Knowledge-sharing and partnership activities such as business and university collaboration are not well developed.

References

European Commission (2010),*EUROPE 2020 A strategy for smart, sustainable and inclusive growth*, Brussels, 3.3.2010 COM (2010) 2020 final.

Kubisz, M. (2011), "Leveraging Training Skills Development in SMEs: An Analysis of Zaglebie Sub-Region, Poland", *OECD Local Economic and Employment Development (LEED) Working Papers*, No. 2011/06, OECD Publishing, Paris, http://dx.doi.org/10.1787/5kgchzjsvnf3-en.

Miranda, G. and G. Larcombe (2012), "Enabling Local Green Growth: Addressing Climate Change Effects on Employment and Local Development", *OECD Local Economic and Employment Development (LEED) Working Papers*, No. 2012/01, OECD Publishing, Paris, http://dx.doi.org/10.1787/5k9h2q92t2r7-en.

Miranda, G. et al. (2011), "Climate Change, Employment and Local Development in Poland", *OECD Local Economic and Employment Development (LEED) Working Papers*, No. 2011/22, OECD Publishing, Paris, http://dx.doi.org/10.1787/5kg0nvfvwjd0-en.

OECD (2014), "SME Survey Questionnaire in Pomorskie, Poland", Paris.

Porter, M.E. and Class van der Linde (1995), "Towards a New Conception of the Environment-Competitiveness Relationship", *Journal of Economic Perspectives*, 9: pp. 97-118.

Stroud, D. et al. (2015), "Governments matter for capitalist economies: Regeneration and transition to green and decent jobs", *Economic and Industrial Democracy*, http://dx.doi.org/10.1177/0143831X15601731, published on 3 September 2015.

Stroud, D. and C. Evans (2014), "Greening steel work: Varieties of capitalism and the 'greening' of skills", *Journal of Education and Work*, http://dx.doi.org/10.1080/13639080.2014.907487, published online 10 April 2014.

Wojewódzki Urząd Pracy w Gdańsku [Provincial Labour Office in Gdańsk] (2013), *Pomorski barometr zawodowy, 2013* [Pomorskie professional barometer, 2013], Gdańsk.

Chapter 5

Skills ecosystem responses

This chapter analyses the training and skills development landscape in Pomorskie, Poland including what programmes and policies have been introduced to address potential skills shortages within the local labour market. Through the identification of which skills are in demand in Pomorskie, training and education policies can be shaped to answer these needs. This chapter looks at how several skills development programmes are supporting the transition to a greener economy. The chapter also draws on lessons learned from coastal areas in other OECD countries which are applicable to Pomorskie. These examples are used to draw conclusions about how to boost the supply of "green" skills in Pomorskie.

Overview

Technological innovations are crucial for the stable and long-term development of the Pomorskie region. Innovations particularly important for the green transformation require advanced scientific skills, referred to as STEM skills (science, technology, engineering, mathematics). Basic skills within these fields include logical reasoning and the capacity to process and find links between data, as well as to identify and solve problems (Bowen, 2012). These highly prized competences – when combined with the business and economic development agendas – help to create long-term jobs and contribute greater added value to the economy (Payne, 2007). Pomorskie can rely on a strong higher education system to respond to skills needs. However, skills shortages are already emerging in blue economy sectors. Continuous vocational education and training and skills ecosystems could be reinforced to better support emerging sectors and career transitions between declining and emerging sectors.

Pomorskie is a strong higher education centre in Northern Poland with specialities in the marine economy sectors

The Pomorskie region is the strongest educational centre in Northern Poland. There are 28 higher education units based in the region and 13 branches of higher education institutions located outside the region. The region's higher education potential is created predominantly by state universities:

- University of Gdańsk – approximately 30 000 students
- Gdańsk University of Technology – approximately 20 000 students
- Medical University of Gdańsk – approximately 5 000 students
- Gdynia Maritime University and the Naval Academy, among others.

The Tri-city agglomeration is one of the leading secondary education centres in Poland. A number of secondary schools in the region have been ranked among the highest quality schools in the country over recent years. They attract the best students from across the country. Nevertheless, analysis of the educational paths of students reveals that the region's higher education system is unable to retain the most talented students, who prefer Poland's main higher education centres in Warsaw or Krakow, or who decide to study abroad (Sagan et al., 2013).

The Pomorskie region has a well-developed higher education system that prepares future employees for the blue economy sectors. The Faculty of Ocean Engineering and Ship Technology at the Technical University of Gdańsk, as well as the Navigation, Entrepreneurship, and Science of Commodities Departments of Gdynia Maritime University offer studies related to transport and logistics. The University of Gdańsk also provides education on transport and logistics, as well oceanography, biology, geology and environmental protection. Other tertiary schools in the Pomorskie region provide education on hydro-engineering, tourism, and other fields related to the exploitation of water resources.

For example, in 2011 there were approximately 4 750 people studying at the TFL (transport, forwarding, logistics) industry-related faculties (out of a total of 100 000 persons studying in the region). The University of Gdańsk, Technical University of Gdańsk and Gdynia Maritime University offer extensive education programmes on foreign trade, logistics, forwarding and port operations. Private universities also offer a wide variety of courses related to the sector. Experts from the TFL sector may also carry out educational activities in secondary-level schools (Invest in Pomerania, 2014).

Skills shortages (especially of highly technical skills) and difficulties retaining talent have already emerged in marine economy sectors

Pomorskie has difficulties retaining talent mainly because of the lack of attractiveness of wages compared to other Western and neighbouring Scandinavian countries. Skills shortages (especially of highly technical skills) have already emerged in blue economy sectors. Pomorskie suffers from a shortage of graduates from fields such as mechatronics and ship systems design (e.g. piping, electricity, furniture). At the same time, biology and biotechnology faculties produce high quality specialists the market is unable to absorb. Many of them decide to emigrate abroad where they find employment in the biotechnology sector. As a result, the high potential of qualified workers – along with the high costs of their biotechnological education – is being drained from the national blue economy. The deficit of bioinformatics specialists is another problem for the biotechnology sector.

Workers with secondary education specific to the offshore industry are a particularly sought after group in the Pomorskie region. As the above analysis reveals, it is difficult to balance demand and supply within the narrow specialities of the blue economy sectors. On one hand, the poor demand for specialised and qualified personnel does not stimulate the development of the education system, while on the other, the research sector related to the blue economy is currently insufficient. As a result, the majority of work provided for foreign contractors consists of assembling elements, rather than producing new, innovative equipment.

According to the research on shipbuilding, carried out for the Regional Labour Office in Gdańsk, the industry seeks welders, workers who prepare and build metal constructions, fitters and operators of plastics manufacturing machines. Professions strictly related to shipbuilding (e.g. Tungsten Inert Gas [TIG] welder, Metal Active Gas [MAG] welder and steel structures cleaner), were listed among the occupations in shortage in the Pomorskie region in the first half of 2013. The soft skills that employers value the most within these professions are diligence, integrity, meticulousness and assiduity. The ability to learn is also an important skill, as the introduction of new technologies and the diversity of services requires workers to be open to acquiring new professional skills. Employers also point to mathematical, scientific and technical competences. This stems from the fact that even the workers who perform typically manual tasks, such as boat builders, painters, carpenters, grinders or hull assemblers, are expected to be able to use project documentation, interpret technical drawings (when working with metal and steel constructions) and isometric drawings (when working with pipe constructions) (Provincial Labour Office in Gdańsk, 2013).

> **Box 5.1. Skills Eco-Systems: The Australian Case**
>
> Australia has developed approaches to workforce development that may well have lessons for the Pomorskie region. A national policy of "Skill Ecosystems Projects" and a regional policy operated in Queensland, the "Skills Formation Strategy", demonstrate how skill formation might be brought within the broader context of labour market and economic development issues. To address an Australian economy increasingly based on low value-added, low skill employment, as well as significant skills shortages and mismatches and an education and training system compromised by unsustainable reforms, a response was required to reinvigorate skill development and utilisation.
>
> A "Skill Eco-Systems" analysis requires understanding of an interconnected web of contextual factors (Buchanan et al., 2001):
>
> - business settings (e.g. the type of product market, competitive strategies, business organisation/networks, financial system)
> - institutional and policy frameworks (VET and non-VET)
> - modes of engaging labour (e.g. labour hire)
> - structure of jobs (e.g. job design and work organisation)
> - level and type of skill formation (e.g. apprenticeships, informal on-the-job training).
>
> The success of the "Skills Ecosystems Projects" and "Skills Formation Strategy" in adopting these principles of skill formation is identified as uneven, but with some notable successes e.g. The "Water Innovation Network Project" created successful networks between researchers, industry VET providers. Such projects are however, identified as difficult to evaluate, require significant lead-time to take root and high levels of trust and co-operation (Payne, 2007). Nevertheless, skills ecosystem approaches focus attention on broader contextual factors. Such strategies are complex and challenging for policy makers, and require thought about the development and deployment of skill in a number of ways. As Payne (2007) identifies it necessitates consideration of the "organisational and competitive strategy of the firm and the wider policy and institutional environment which shape firms' choices and behaviour(s)". The Australian government's "Green Skills Agreement" (2009) develops this strand of thinking into policy aims for building capacity into vocational education and training practice to deliver the necessary sustainability skills for greening industry, and particularly the re-skilling of vulnerable workers (Fairbrother, P. et al., 2012).

The identified skill shortages in the shipbuilding sector could become an important bottleneck to seize emerging economic opportunities from the green economy. It is projected, that within the next two decades, Polish shipyards may find prospects for development in constructing vessels for petroleum and gas mining, and for off-shore wind power stations (Institute for Market Economics, 2010). Even though the development of the wind energy sector is more advanced in Denmark, Sweden, and Germany rather, Polish shipyards are ready to build vessels for wind turbine installation and maintenance.

After shipbuilding, transport and logistics appear to offer the best prospects for development and the generation of jobs in the region. Research by the Regional Labour Office in Gdańsk reveals that the most valued competency in this area of business is responsibility, followed by integrity and diligence. Freight forwarders should demonstrate soft skills, i.e. interpersonal relations and propriety. Employees in this sector are expected to have vocationally-oriented education, or in some cases, to be secondary economic technical school graduates. Knowledge of foreign languages and the ability to use information and communication technologies are crucial. Lack of English language skills disqualifies potential candidates for freight forwarders. The candidates should also have additional competences (e.g. customs agent) and take specialised training courses.

Key professions related to maritime transport also have their specific requisites. Potential employees are expected to have officers' licenses issued by the Maritime Office and a list of competences and qualifications (e.g. radio, fire-fighting certificates, and individual rescue techniques). Language skills are equally important. Although English is crucial, knowledge of Norwegian and Spanish is also useful (Provincial Labour Office in Gdańsk, 2013). The potential jobs created in the maritime tourism sector will probably have a lesser impact on Pomorskie's labour market than the ones generated by transport and logistics. There is a deficit of freight trans-shipping and navigation services technical workers, while the supply and demand of labour in the tourism sector remains more or less balanced.

The response of higher education institutions to the skills needs of the green economy

The skills ecosystem's role in assisting the greening of the economy is mainly driven by the higher education system. The creation of new jobs in the green economy sector is mostly shaped by vocational and higher education (Lewandowski and Magda, 2014). Both private and public schools in Poland have developed curricula in relation to environmental protection. There are two popular profiles of graduates: environmental engineering and environmental public administration (Miranda et al., 2011a; Miranda et al., 2011b).

A successful initiative linked to the labour market to attract students and raise interest in studies related to the green economy was the launch of the ordered courses programme in fields selected by the Ministry of Science and Higher Education at national level. The studies were financed by EU structural funds in 2007-2013. The students enrolled on this programme received a scholarship, which significantly raised interest in the selected fields of education. As part of the programme some specialisations were opened in fields that were in demand from potential employers. Mechatronics, which was launched in 2009 at Gdańsk University of Technology, is one such case (Politechnika Gdańska, 2015d). There was also a specialisation in the field of renewable energy.

The programme was successful in increasing young people's interest in studying science and technology and in strengthening the co-operation between universities and enterprises. Nevertheless, it had weaknesses, as graduates in some fields, (in particular graduates in environmental protection), had difficulties finding a job in their field afterwards (Górniak, 2013). This tends to demonstrate that the labour market demand for skills related to the green economy is still weak.

In 2015, the Ministry of Science and Higher Education announced the replacement of the ordered courses programme with the "Competency Development Programme". The programme will be aimed at strengthening entrepreneurship education, professional, interpersonal and analytical competences. The new programme will support the use of modern teaching methods such as workshops, the use of new technologies in higher education and the promotion of modular education as well as interdisciplinary studies. The programme is an opportunity to better match education profiles to the requirements of innovative forms of business and entrepreneurship. This could be beneficial to the transition to a green economy.

The role of the education system in assisting the transition to a green economy is increasingly being recognised and the higher education system is adapting to this change. The accessibility of EU funds dedicated to the development of green technologies, positive changes in the regulatory framework such as the recently adopted Law on Renewable Energy Sources and new educational initiatives are gaining prominence. The introduction of the Renewable Energy Law paves the way for the creation of thousands of micro-installations which, in turn, will stimulate greater demand for designers and technicians to serve their needs. For several years Gdańsk University of Technology has been delivering courses on technologies that use renewable energy sources. Their curriculum includes such aspects as designing and selecting equipment for the needs of green energy technologies (Politechnika Gdańska, 2015a).

Another positive example of changes in higher education in Pomorskie is the opening of a new course at the Gdańsk University of Technology in 2015: Green Technologies and Monitoring. The new field of study replaces two earlier ones: Environmental Protection and Management (EPM) and Technologies of Environmental Protection (TOŚ) (Politechnika Gdańska, 2015b). The aim of restructuring of provided courses is to better adjust the education to growing needs of the green economy. Gdańsk University of Technology also organises seminars and training on green solutions. One such example is the Green Houses training organised by the Foundation for Energy-Efficient Constructions at the Faculty of Architecture, dedicated to technologies and innovative solutions in construction (Politechnika Gdańska 2015c).

The creation of the Business and Green Technology course at the Faculty of Economics, University of Gdańsk (Uniwersytet Gdański, 2015) also demonstrates changes in the higher education system. The objective of the course is to equip its graduates with practical knowledge, skills and competences in the fields of economics, environmental protection and green technologies. The graduates are expected to acquire skills in:

- elaborating comprehensive green business concepts, as well as technological and commercial plans for green enterprises and initiatives
- assessing the economic situation of green enterprises and indicating fields for improving their activities
- planning and organising basic economic processes for enterprises working with green solutions
- operating green equipment and installations, as well as managing enterprises specialising in this field.

In view of the emerging changes, continuous attention to training the trainers is also important to address the needs of a transition towards a green economy. During the interviews, representatives of academia pointed out that increasing funding for the exchange of international researchers was also necessary to sustain the growth of academic staff's competences and knowledge. Inviting leading, world-recognised researchers, even for short periods of time, was deemed to be particularly effective and beneficial and can have a significant impact on the level of studies and education at the universities.

Secondary education is also beginning to witness changes in terms of teaching professions related to green technologies. For example, Gdańsk Power Engineering School offers vocational education for future renewable energy systems and installation technicians. Graduates of this course receive qualifications in the assembly and operation of renewable energy equipment and systems (Gdańsk, 2015).

A limited response from public employment services, continuing education and training programmes

There is no specific element related to greening skills in Pomorskie's employment and continuing education systems. Blue economy and water sectors are addressed within broader programmes but not as stand-alone programmes. For example, the Regional Labour Office in Gdańsk implements support programmes for new entrants into the labour market, older workers and the socially excluded but does not have a dedicated programme addressing green skills. In addition, there is no specific programme to assist with career transitions from declining sectors towards new and emerging sectors.

This is all the more problematic as laid off workers from the traditional blue economy sectors could be included in programmes for the unemployed, which provide apprenticeships for new jobs that often require only basic skills. The conversion of traditional jobs to greener jobs could therefore take place mainly through training courses organised within the companies in this apprenticeship system, or through alternative skills development mechanisms. In other countries, specialised training programmes have been at the heart of local initiatives to boost skills in important sectors such as the renewable energy sector for instance the CENIFER foundation for renewable energies in Navarra, Spain or the Academy of the future project in Flanders (see Box 5.2).

> **Box 5.2. Skills anticipation and training for renewable energy in Navarra and Flanders**
>
> **CENIFER, Navarra, Spain**
>
> Navarre region has undergone over the last years a fast development of renewable energy. Between 1994, when there was no renewable energy production in Navarre, and 2009 the region expanded its electricity production from renewable sources to 65% including 993 MW of wind power and almost 100 MW of photovoltaic power. The region has seen a rise in demand for renewable energy specialists, including wind power maintenance staff and was initially confronted with a lack of skilled workers. Wind power maintenance requires mechanical or electrical training or an engineering background, which usually involves technical skills such as electric and mechanic connections, tools use, electric controls and plan interpreting.
>
> In this context, the CENIFER foundation was set up as a public sector initiative with the goal of delivering skills training for renewable energy. CENIFER now offers a wide range of renewable energy courses, including a wind power maintenance course delivering training in the skills needed for this new occupation. The foundation also organises training for trainers (technical updates) and participates in international programmes.
>
> Thanks to CENIFER, Navarre has been able to cover the jobs needed for this new occupation, facilitating the rapid expansion of renewable energy production in the region. One key reason for success was that the skills response was adapted to companies' needs in particular SMEs with courses of short duration with a strong practical element.

> **Box 5.2. Skills anticipation and training for renewable energy in Navarra and Flanders** *(cont.)*
>
> **The Academy for the future project in Flanders**
>
> The Academy of the future project in Flanders aims to help address skills needs in the blue energy sector (offshore wind energy parks). In 2013, a lack of technical employees was identified for the sector. The academy of the future helped mapping demand and supply with the input from the Flanders' maritime cluster (FMC), an interest group of large and small companies active in marine or maritime business. It was identified that workers would require specific skills: language (English or German), technical, autonomy as well as on health and safety. A new professional profile linked to offshore wind (e.g. welding for windmills) was created. The Academy collaborated with Syntra west, the Flemish training agency, university colleges and with private trainers. Trainings will start next April-May 2015 provided the overarching policy framework promoting off-shore wind (Plan Stevin) is implemented.
>
> *Source:* OECD, 2017.

The new "Competency Development Programme" for 2014-2020 established by the Polish Ministry of Science may be considered as an attempt to balance the supply and demand of adequately qualified college graduates to fill labour market needs. The emphasis of this new programme is on skills to increase the chances of graduates in the labour market and reduce unemployment. However there are no mechanisms to anticipate green skills set up at national or regional level. In Pomorskie, a regional labour market observatory does exist but does not specifically monitor the greening of skills and jobs.

The new Polish European Social Fund Operational Programme "Knowledge, Education and Development 2014-2020" could help to set up new mechanisms to better anticipate skills for greening blue economy sectors. For example, it could help to establish a Programme Board or sectoral competencies boards to collaborate with entrepreneurs in estimating the demand for specific occupations in relation to greening the economy, and targeting blue economy sectors. The boards could also participate in the creation of training networks involving entrepreneurs as well as social partners (Lewandowski and Magda 2014).

The creation of new institutions, such as Programme Board and sectoral competencies boards, in accordance with the Operational Programme (*Wiedza Edukacja Rozwój na lata 2014-2020*), seems to be justified. The scope of their actions would cover, among others, collaboration with the entrepreneurs in estimating the demand for specific occupations. Hence, their actions would include the evaluation of demand within the green and the blue economies. The aforementioned Boards could participate in the creation of training networks involving entrepreneurs as well as the social partners (Lewandowski and Magda 2014).

Limited knowledge-sharing activities between education and businesses

According to the interviews carried out for this report, local entrepreneurs' opinion on the level of higher education in Pomorskie is relatively good, although collaboration between education and businesses is not very well developed. Participants in the project roundtable noted that a number of institutional, structural and cultural barriers existed to building links between business and researchers in Pomorskie. Often, research results or ideas do not reach the business sector due to a lack of information flow. Both groups have very different objectives and cultures, in particular the way in which information is used for innovation, i.e. open source vs commercially confident. The academic evaluation system does not currently incentivise co-operation or exchange of ideas with the business sector. Intermediaries could help to reconcile both worlds and overcome this "clash of cultures". This would require training and specific skill sets e.g. business experience, scientific training, and negotiation skills.

The Pomeranian Regional Chamber of Commerce (*Regionalna Izba Gospodarcza Pomorza*), the Employers of Pomerania (*Pracodawcy Pomorza*), and the Pomeranian Chamber of Crafts for Small and Medium Enterprises (*Pomorska Izba Rzemieślnicza Małych i Średnich Przedsiębiorstw*) could play this intermediary role and create a bridge between the entrepreneurs, science and specialised education sectors. They have the capabilities to efficiently inform, train, and encourage experiments and innovative implementations – especially among SMEs.

Industry clusters or collaboration platforms between businesses are also limited in Pomorskie, despite some examples in the blue economy sectors, such as the Maritime Cluster that benefitted from an international collaboration within the Interregional Maritime Cluster InterMareC between 2003 and 2007. Pomorskie was represented by the Pomerania Development Agency SA, which co-ordinated the actions of seven regional institutions: Maritime Institute in Gdańsk, Ship Design and Research Centre SA, Institute of Oceanography at the University of Gdańsk, Institute of Hydro-Engineering of the Polish Academy of Sciences, Maritime Office in Gdynia, Gdynia Shipyard SA and GEOMOR-NIVA Geoscience and Marine Research & Consulting Sp. z o.o (Agencja Rozwoju Pomorza, 2014). A Polish Maritime Cluster currently operates in Pomorskie and incorporates scientists from the Gdynia Maritime University.

The survey of firms carried out in Pomorskie confirms that training is crucial for entrepreneurs to implement green measures in their businesses. OECD studies (2014) show that employers have a critical role to play in the provision and design of employment and training programmes to better match the supply of skills to demand. Several interviewees (Pomeranian Regional Chamber of Commerce, managers from the energy and shipbuilding sector) are not satisfied with the quality of training programmes offered. In 2013, the training programmes financed by public funds such as the Labour Fund or the European Social Fund were evaluated as particularly low quality in the Pomorskie Professional Barometer (Provincial Labour Office in Gdańsk, 2013). The public funds related to training programmes are predominantly distributed to companies that specialise in generic training rather than those that could provide specific professional training. Training programmes are mainly targeted at low qualified workers and offer only basic knowledge and skills. The fact that these training programmes do not correspond to entrepreneurs' needs in relation to innovation or green economy skills was identified as a problem by entrepreneurs in the interviews and also appeared in public debates related to the allocation of EU funding for Poland during the period between 2014 and 2020.

Employers should continuously collaborate with the public sector on increasing the efficiency of the education and training system. The information flow between the local government sector that organises the EU funded training programmes and the companies that could benefit from them was also identified as insufficient. This is confirmed by survey results, as one third of companies mentioned the lack of information on available training programmes as a major obstacle. The survey also shows that many entrepreneurs expect training to be carried out on the job. Business organisations and technological institutes are trusted partners and could play a more prominent role in organising training programmes for the blue economy sectors. During the interviews, business representatives made several suggestions on how the expansion of the skills base in order to assist the green transition:

- Introduce common subsidies for green jobs in the companies funded by labour offices. These funds could finance the work of employees to train apprentices. Employers from the sector stress that they bear the excessively high costs of employing apprentices, even though they receive aid from labour offices for this purpose. As the activities in this sector are technologically highly advanced, the cost of apprenticeships for particular jobs is a significant barrier. Subsidies should also be extended to enable workers to train educators and not exclusively fund apprenticeships.
- Introduce a mechanism for students to undertake unpaid work during the final year of their studies.
- Consider introducing the "2 x 2" system during the final years of vocational and secondary school education and in universities, i.e. 2 months of education at school, 2 months of work at a company.

Conclusions

Pomorskie is a strong educational centre for the blue economy sectors. In particular, higher education (the University of Gdańsk and University of Gdynia) has specialised curricula for the blue economy and is increasing its education offer related to the green economy. Nevertheless, skills shortages are already being identified in blue economy sectors and the region has difficulties attracting and retaining talent in research activities.

In addition, major challenges have been identified in Pomorskie in relation to the skills ecosystems response to the transition to a greener economy. There is limited attention to skills needs emerging from the transition to a greener economy in continuing education or in employment services. A regional labour market observatory does exist but does not incorporate green aspects into its work. There is no specific programme provided by the employment services to target the greening potential of the blue economy sectors.

The allocation of new European funds for Poland, within the framework of the cohesion policy 2014-2020, generated a discussion on dedicating such funds for human capital development. During the open public debate doubts were raised regarding the efficiency of the use of funds in the previous Financial Perspective. The interviews conducted confirmed the prevalence of this opinion. It was pointed out that, in many cases, the publicly financed courses carried out by training companies did not fulfil the expectations of the people and enterprises to whom they were addressed, and that the largest beneficiaries of these programmes were the training companies themselves. Research also identified an insufficient flow of information between the local government sector that organises EU funded training programmes and the companies that could benefit from such programmes. The survey results revealed that one third of companies think there is a lack of information on available training programmes.

Knowledge-sharing activities between education and businesses, or between businesses themselves, are also limited. Collaboration with entrepreneurs is not encouraged. There are no initiatives to create intermediaries to lead reflection and to assist businesses in creating a vision for sustainability and the green economy. However, there is a network of associations such as the Pomeranian Regional Chamber of Commerce, the Employers of Pomerania, and the Pomeranian Chamber of Crafts for Small and Medium Enterprises that could play a more prominent role and facilitate such activities.

References

Agencja Rozwoju Pomorza (2014), *Agencja Rozwoju Pomorza*, www.arp.gda.pl/, (accessed 28 October 2014).

Bowen, A. (2012), "Green Growth, Green Jobs and Labor Markets",*Policy Research Paper*, no. 5990, Washington, DC: World Bank.

Buchanan, J. et al. (2001), *Beyond Flexibility: Skills and Work in the Future*, Sydney: New South Wales Board of Vocational Education and Training.

Fairbrother, P. et al. (2012), *Jobs and Skills Transition for the Latrobe Valley: Phase 1: Benchmark occupations and skill sets*, RMIT University and Swinburne University of Technology, ISBN 978-1-921-91673-1.

Gdańsk (2015), *www.gdansk.pl*, www.gdansk.pl/e-poradnik_gimnazjalisty,1711,25290.html (accessed 25 March 2015).

Górniak, J. (2013), *Youth or experience? Human capital in Poland*, Polish Agency for Enterprise Development and Jagiellonian University, Warsaw-Cracow, https://en.parp.gov.pl/images/PARP_publications/pdf/2013_bkl_youth_or_experience_en.pdf.

Instytut Badań nad Gospodarką Rynkową [Institute for Market Economics] (2010), "Stan obecny i prognoza zmian oraz kierunków rozwoju gospodarki i rynku pracy w województwie pomorskim", *Prognozy i scenariusze do roku 2020, Raport podsumowujący II etap badania pt* ["The present state and predict changes and directions of development of the economy and the labour market in Pomerania", Forecasts and Scenarios to 2020, A summary report Phase II study], Gdańsk.

Invest in Pomerania (2014), *Invest in Pomerania*, www.investinpomerania.pl (accessed 28 October 2014).

Lewandowski, P. and I. Magda (2014), *Employment in Poland – Labour in the Age of Structural Change*, Warsaw.

Miranda, G. et al. (2011a), "Climate Change, Employment and Local Development in Poland", *OECD Local Economic and Employment Development (LEED) Working Papers*, No. 2011/22, OECD Publishing, Paris, http://dx.doi.org/10.1787/5kg0nvfuwjd0-en.

Miranda, G. et al. (2011b), "Climate Change, Employment and Local Development, Sydney, Australia", *OECD Local Economic and Employment Development (LEED) Working Papers*, No. 2011/14, OECD Publishing, Paris, http://dx.doi.org/10.1787/5kg20639kgkj-en.

OECD (2017), *Boosting Skills for Greener Jobs in Flanders, Belgium*, OECD Publishing, Paris, http://dx.doi.org/10.1787/9789264265264-en.

OECD (2014), *Employment and Skills Strategies in Northern Ireland, United Kingdom*, OECD Publishing, Paris, http://dx.doi.org/10.1787/9789264208872-en.

Payne, J. (2007), "Skills in context: what can the UK learn from Australia's skill ecosystem projects?" *SKOPE Research Paper*, No. 70.

Politechnika Gdańska (2015a), *Energetyka międzywydziałowa*, http://oio.pg.edu.pl/energetyka-miedzywydzialowa (accessed 9 June 2017).

Politechnika Gdańska (2015b), *Faculty of Chemistry*, http://chem.pg.edu.pl/en (accessed 9 June 2017).

Politechnika Gdańska (2015c), *Wydział Architektury*, http://arch.pg.edu.pl/ (accessed 9 June 2017).

Politechnika Gdańska (2015d), *Kształcenie zamawiane na kierunku mechatronikana Wydziale Mechanicznym Politechniki Gdańskiej*, http://mech.pg.edu.pl/pl/rekrutacja/kierunek-zamawiany-mechatronika (accessed 9 June 2017).

Sagan, I., C. Martinez-Fernandez and T. Weyman (2013), "Pomorskie Region: Responding to Demographic Transitions Towards 2035", *OECD Local Economic and Employment Development (LEED) Working Papers*, No. 2013/07, OECD Publishing, Paris, http://dx.doi.org/10.1787/5k48189zpsmw-en.

Uniwersytet Gdański (2015), *Biznes i technologia ekologiczna*, http://ug.edu.pl/rekrutacja/studia/kierunki_studiow/20162017/biznes_i_technologia_ekologiczna-stacjonarne-ii_stopnia (accessed 9 June 2017).

Wojewódzki Urząd Pracy w Gdańsku [Provincial Labour Office in Gdańsk] (2013), *Pomorski barometr zawodowy, 2013* [Pomorskie professional barometer, 2013], Gdańsk.

Chapter 6

Policy recommendations

This chapter provides key recommendations related to boosting the supply of skills in blue economy sectors in Pomorskie, Poland. Through identification of what skills are in demand, Pomorskie can increase growth in the blue economy. Boosting these skills will support businesses to develop more sustainable production processes to further the transition to a greener local economy. Within Pomorskie, more can be done to better articulate a vision for the green economy within blue economy sectors, assist businesses in seizing opportunities to green sectors, encourage knowledge sharing in collaboration with businesses, and leverage the use of European Social Funds for skills training activities. With these strategies in mind, actors at the local and national level can coordinate the governance of these policies to maximize the growth of Poland's blue economy at the local level.

Key recommendations

The research and consultations with stakeholders from Pomorskie identified a variety of initiatives concerned with furthering the transition to a green economy. However, this report finds that policy makers could pursue a more coherent and integrated strategy to the employment and skills dimensions of the shift to more sustainable production and development. In particular, the recommendations outlined here highlight the need to co-ordinate efforts between stakeholders, including businesses, training providers and government actors, in order to more effectively promote sustainable growth and development in the region.

Better articulating a vision for the green economy within marine economy sectors

The Polish national and regional frameworks for addressing the green economy have greatly evolved in the past decades. The importance of tackling environmental issues is recognised in many national, regional and sectorial policy instruments related to blue economy sectors. Nevertheless, the transition to a green economy could benefit from a more-clearly defined vision and precise delivery instruments. Some recent developments such as the adoption of the "Law on renewable energy sources" are likely to facilitate investments in green energy infrastructure. A better articulation of the green economy vision for blue economy sectors is needed with clear implications for spatial planning. The development of a blue economy in Pomorskie undoubtedly constitutes an opportunity. It requires strategic, long-term actions and planning that, in turn, depend particularly on stable political and governance structures. This requires a multilevel and multi-governance approach which promotes horizontal and vertical collaboration, integration and strategic thinking.

Recommendation: Improve overall governance and co-ordination of the blue economy. This includes strengthening strategic partnerships with neighbour regions to co-ordinate marine social planning and blue economy strategies

The report and interviews highlighted the complexity of the current decision-making framework for the blue economy and ocean and water resources exploitation. Responsibilities are dispersed and collaboration between various ministries remains limited (e.g. the responsibility for managing the Lower Vistula is spread among six different ministries). This creates delays and administrative burden. Twenty eight per cent of interviewed companies consider administrative barriers as a major obstacle to greening business practices in blue economy sectors. This report shows that Poland has already taken preliminary steps to boost blue economy sectors in particular through a sector approach instead of through the development of a comprehensive multi-sector strategy. The engagement of the Industrial Development Agency in the offshore sector is a good example.

This approach risks overlooking opportunities in emerging sectors. For instance, while numerous policy documents address specific sectors such as shipbuilding, fisheries, maritime natural resources exploitation, energy sector or maritime tourism, opportunities in smaller emerging sectors such as biotechnology or aquaculture are not given focus. It also reduces the likelihood of the development of a clear long-term plan, which addresses potential conflicts and builds synergies between various sectors. In addition, the land and maritime areas are treated as two separate entities with the control and management executed by different bodies. This makes rational exploitation and management of coastal areas challenging. The majority of innovative and environmentally friendly sectors of the blue economy operate in coastal zones or strongly depend on the functional exploitation of land and water areas.

An instrument such as spatial planning which take into account potential synergies and conflicts between various sectors could help. So far, the maritime areas were not subject to the spatial planning policies as occurred in land areas. Only recently have actions been taken and a pilot plan developed. The development and co-functioning of economic activities such as tourism, offshore wind energy, seabed resources extraction, aquaculture or transport within the limited area of national waters requires a spatial development plan, as the conflicts between these functions may block their development.

Strong relationships with national and international levels of government can help support a regional innovation system for the blue economy in Pomorskie. The participation of Polish and Pomorskie stakeholders in international forums, such as the EU multi-sectoral maritime stakeholder platform for the Baltic Sea, should be supported. The objective is not only to strengthen international collaboration but also to contribute to building strong institutional links between Polish regional authorities, universities and research institutes as well as regional enterprises through their joint participation.

Recommendation: Better monitor the skills-related aspects of the transition to a green economy, particularly for blue economy sectors

This reports highlights that there is currently no system set up in Poland to monitor the labour market impacts of the transition to a greener economy. An approach which encourages both local and sector dimensions such as the National Observatory on Green Skills and Jobs in France could help Polish regions and blue economy sectors to better anticipate and prepare future skills responses. This is particularly relevant for traditional blue economy sectors such as shipbuilding. This type of observatory could facilitate the early identification of career pathways for displaced workers into new emerging sectors.

The creation of new institutions, such as the Programme Board and sectoral competencies boards, in accordance with the *Wiedza Edukacja Rozwój na lata 2014-2020* Operational Programme, could also be created. The scope of their actions could cover, among others, collaboration with entrepreneurs and local businesses in estimating the demand for labour and jobs in specific occupations. Additionally, their scope of action could also include an evaluation of demand within the green and the blue economies. The aforementioned Boards could participate in the creation of training networks involving entrepreneurs as well as the social partners (Lewandowski and Magda, 2014).

> **Box 6.1. National observatory on green skills and jobs France**
>
> The French Observatory for Green Skills and Jobs (ONEMEV) is a structure for dialogue and work among various stakeholders which is co-ordinated by the French General Commission for Sustainable development. It aims to build a methodological framework to conduct studies and collect data and ensure a shared diagnosis on jobs, professions and training for green growth. It produces an annual review of its activity including a synthesis of the results of this observation.
>
> ONEMEV has several working themes – one of which brings together regional observatories for training, employment and other local stakeholders to develop methods and tools for collecting comparable regional data on economic activities, occupations and jobs linked to the green economy, socio-demographic evolutions, recruitment process and types, skills and training needs to meet companies' requirements and assist career transitions.
>
> *Source:* OECD, 2017.

Recommendation: Integrate and streamline governance structures for shared water assets at the local level

This report highlights that the policy framework for the blue economy and water management sectors is fragmented at both the regional and national level. The governance structure is complex, involving several ministries and administration bodies. The competences of the Regional Environmental Protection and Water Fund are limited exclusively to land areas and do not extend beyond the shoreline. The seabed is managed by the Polish Geological Institute while the water column is under the jurisdiction of Maritime Offices. Many interviewees have argued that the strict, formally-institutional division is undermining economic activities in these areas. They also report conflicts and obstacles to the development of the hydro-power sector, river transport, renewable energy and tourism linked to the designation of Natura 2000 sites. Nevertheless, this report shows that the changes underway to reinforce policy instruments could bring a more holistic approach for instance with the use of maritime spatial planning. The Maritime Institute of Gdańsk is preparing a study on the determinants of spatial planning of Polish maritime areas. This could be complemented by a more precise mapping of the current and underrepresented sectors such as blue biotechnology. Improved articulation of common goals, including linking the use of waters, rivers, coasts and marine assets into an integrated strategy, could also be effective.

Recommendation: Further explore the role of the blue economy sectors as a "smart specialisation" mechanism for Pomorskie at the local level

The development of blue economy sectors could form the basis for a "smart specialisation" strategy for the Pomorskie region. This approach would combine industrial, educational and innovation policies on a limited number of priority areas for knowledge-based investments, focusing on a region's strengths and comparative advantages (OECD, 2013). This report shows how several blue economy sectors present a strong development potential for the region. They also present opportunities for assisting the region to transition to a greener economy. Tourism presents a high potential for sustainable growth in the region. Although a wide range of touristic activities are available in Pomorskie such as cruises and sailing, new tourist activities such as fishing could be further developed

Tri-city is the second strongest biotechnology centre in the country after Warsaw and a national leader in researching innovative forms of ecosystem services development. However, the lack of collaboration with industry and a lack of funds for demonstration projects and practical application limit the development of these sectors. Frequently, such technologies developed in Pomorskie are not implemented in the region but exported abroad.

In the shipbuilding sector, the implementation of green measures could be related to reducing noise emissions and fuel consumption. Lowering fuel consumption contributes in the long-term to decreasing the costs of operating ships. This increasingly motivates the ship owners to introduce green technologies. However, given the costs of such measures, companies are unlikely to take action without a national regulatory obligation. Building on this research, Pomorskie authorities should explore further with regional stakeholders the possibility of selecting "blue economy" as a smart specialisation sector. This may help to securing further investments and support for the blue economy sectors.

Assist businesses in seizing opportunities to green traditional as well as emerging sectors

The survey of companies shows that the majority of businesses in blue economy sectors in Pomorskie still consider environmental challenges as minor and the transition to the green economy as a cumbersome and legally-demanding process. Awareness of the benefits and opportunities of the green economy is still limited. Assistance to small and medium sized companies in dealing with complex administrative requirements emerging from environmental regulation would also help the switch to a more positive business mind-set. This requires a comprehensive set of actions to promote innovation with awareness raising, dedicated funds, and support to business clusters, incubators and other forms of dedicated support to SMEs. Newfoundland and Labrador in Canada has adopted similar comprehensive strategies to promote innovation in rural area.

Recommendation: Support business cluster activities in the blue economy sector at the regional level. This includes supporting a green economy incubator to promote entrepreneurship in traditional or emerging blue economy sectors

The company survey highlighted the limited involvement of companies in business clusters. Less than one in five businesses interviewed reported collaborating with a business cluster or industry association to keep abreast of developments and innovation in their sector. Collaboration with university, local government or foreign partners is also negligible (less than 5%). Knowledge, common contacts and information flows are vital elements of innovation policies. Such networks can help disseminate good practices and mobilise investments in green economy projects. At the roundtable, there was a clear acknowledgement by key stakeholders that finding effective means and support for the exchange of information and technological expertise is imperative, particularly at the sector level. An absence of clearly defined organisational, communication, administrative and legal infrastructures for engaging in knowledge sharing was noted.

There are examples of cluster activities that could be strengthened in the blue economy sectors, such as the Maritime Cluster that benefitted from an international collaboration within the Interregional Maritime Cluster InterMareC between 2003 and 2007. A Polish Maritime Cluster currently operates in Pomorskie and incorporates scientists from the Gdynia Maritime University. Business participation should be encouraged. Regional authorities could act as a facilitator for the cluster and set up and exchange information on blue economy resources.

> Box 6.2. **Comprehensive innovation and skills strategies in Newfoundland and Labrador, Canada**
>
> The Department of Innovation, Business and Rural Development in Newfoundland and Labrador (Canada) is responsible for ocean technology, regional development, trade and export activities, innovation, strategic industries and business development. It has a corporate office in the capital city and 5 regional offices in 17 field or satellite offices. This structure allows the department to engage at the local level with communities and to communicate to provide direct programmes and service on a daily basis.
>
> The department supports programmes that invest in infrastructure, capacity building, research and marketing, and tries to develop suppliers and build capacity within small and medium enterprises (SMEs) and non-governmental organisations (NGOs). This presents a real opportunity, since small businesses can become part of the supply chain by getting the tools they need to become competitive and learning how to work in some of the regional industries.
>
> The regional government plays a significant role as a facilitator, bringing the stakeholders together to try to give communities the tools they need to make regional development happen.
>
> Regional development in Newfoundland and Labrador involves empowering citizens to make things happen in their communities, and providing them with the necessary confidence and tools to become leaders. This might include, for example, working with women entrepreneurs for training in business-to-business communication and developing the skills and confidence they need to be able to work in a business-to-business environment. Skills transfers and retraining have been very important in the regional economy. Since traditional industries have closed, the province has had to work with displaced workers on retraining and transferring skills.
>
> Working with neighbouring universities, the department has developed sectorial strategies and place-based training to try to meet industry's needs.
>
> A cluster approach has been adopted to develop infrastructure focused on certain opportunities, such as the health sector. Investments with colleges have made it possible to offer specific programmes in health and social sciences. In addition, to attract immigrants, many temporary workers have been recruited into the economy.
>
> Finally, the department's mandate is to support the growth and expansion of SMEs. Integration and co-ordination among government authorities is critical, since many departments in the provincial government have some responsibility for labour market development. Intra-governmental co-ordination has helped ensure that the various resources available are being used. Access to capital is a primary consideration for SMEs, but more than money is at stake. To create vibrant enterprises, much is required: improving cluster development, increasing the capacity for innovation, positioning companies to participate in the global economy, access to high-quality education and good-quality public infrastructure.
>
> *Source:* OECD, 2014c.

This platform could ensure stakeholder dialogue at several levels, establishing an agenda for the collaboration of national government, universities and business associations, setting up a data collection tool or taskforce, for instance a database of blue economy initiatives and how they can be steered towards a greener economy. A database could provide the newest research on current and future demand for products and services offered by the Polish offshore sector, the newest geological research, innovative solutions introduced around the world, the implementation of legal acts on the European level, the directions of work on future regulations. Strategic planning in the maritime sector could also be one of the tasks of the exchange platform.

Business incubators could provide the infrastructure and expertise to improve collaboration, particularly in green-blue economy sectors. Some of the features could entail affordable business space, technical assistance and developing collaboration between companies operating in similar fields. A blue economy technology accelerator, similar to the Polish Greenevo project, could be used to develop the sector at the regional level. Similar assistance, such as support, tools, marketing and branding, specialist training courses, protection of industrial intellectual property could be developed in a public-private partnership.

Recommendation: Raise awareness of the benefits of the green economy and continue to reduce the administrative burden associated with "greening" industries. Mobilise public funding to support green innovation in blue economy sectors

The OECD survey of local companies shows that the majority of businesses consider environmental challenges as rather minor. This is particularly the case for the protection of biodiversity and air quality (close to 70% of respondents consider these issues to be minor challenges). To address this challenge, activities that increase the visibility of companies that are taking proactive steps to green their business practice and raise the profile of Pomorskie in relation to its unique natural assets could help raise awareness among businesses.

Although the process for Environment Impact Assessments (EIA) has improved drastically with the new policy framework, business representatives, in particular in the field of hydro-power and water transport, have stressed that the implementation of EIA and Natura 2000 remain an obstacle to the development of blue economy sectors. This suggests that improvements and simplifications for instance with harmonized methodologies are still possible (OECD, 2015).

According to over 60% of the respondents in the company survey, the most important barrier to greening company practices is the perceived high costs or the lack of financing. This is particularly emphasised by representatives of small companies that employ between 10 and 49 persons. In this context, it is therefore crucial that appropriate public financing support be geared towards the green economy transition. According to interviewees, the lack of available financing instruments is a considerable obstacle to the development of innovation in biotechnology, aquaculture and other ecosystem services.

Establishing a dedicated fund for greening businesses and accelerating the uptake of new business models similar to approaches in Denmark could help support green innovation in Pomorskie. Public support could also pilot test activities that have been done in Denmark and Scotland.

6. POLICY RECOMMENDATIONS

> **Box 6.3. Supporting green business development and business models**
>
> **A dedicated fund, the example of Denmark**
>
> The Fund for Green Business Development promotes eco-efficiency in Danish firms by giving grants to selected firms. The fund holds around 19 million Euros for the period 2013-2016. It supports innovative projects with potential for creating growth and new green jobs in Denmark and acts as catalysts for environmental improvements.
>
> The Fund has also joined forces with the Danish Regions and the Regional Municipality of Bornholm to establish an accelerator programme on green business model innovation. The programme was launched in October 2014. The programme recognises as a starting point that with new business models, "companies can conquer new markets and customer segments as well as increasing their competitiveness". The Fund supports businesses in an initial phase to develop an overall business plan. The Danish regions and municipalities assist businesses in a second phase for testing and implementing the new business model.
>
> **Testing facilities in Denmark and Scotland**
>
> The creation of testing facilities, as in the Shetland Islands (Scotland) and Region Sjælland (Denmark), where producers can verify the performance of their new apparatus, is a form of R&D activity that can assist local businesses in developing new green products.
>
> In Shetland, a group of researchers have experimented with storage systems to lower the cost of generating, storing and supplying hydrogen for power units.
>
> In Region Sjælland, the municipality of Lolland is experimenting in operation and maintenance for wind turbines, and hydrogen-based storage systems.
>
> *Source:* Grøn Omstilling, 2015; OECD, 2012.

The survey results reveal that the most desired form of aid from public authorities to help companies green their business is investment support for purchasing machines and equipment, as well as financial incentives that support the employment of new workers. Support should be tailored to the needs of the sector. The interviews with blue economy sectors representatives highlight that there are different expectations in various sectors concerning public support. These differences should be taken into account.

In the energy sector, stakeholders reported a need for specific support to innovative SMEs that currently lack access to funding as national financial support is largely directed to large enterprise groups with large scale projects. In the biotechnology sector, the Pomorskie region possesses high scientific and research potential that remains unexploited. Strengthening the sector could be achieved by seeking foreign companies to invest in Pomorskie (e.g. via regional authorities' initiative Invest in Pomerania) and introducing financial incentives for the enterprises to invest in R&D. In aquaculture, the development of ecosystem services such as using mussels for water purification or – although still economically unviable – using algae for biomass production could be promoted.

Promoting skills and knowledge sharing in collaboration with businesses

The survey highlighted that there is a strong skills dimension of the transition to a greener economy. While companies do not frequently mention skills shortages and gaps as a major obstacle to greening their practices, 65% of Pomorskie's companies that have implemented green measures in their business practices had to address the issue of skills. They did so by hiring consultancy services (40% of companies that implemented green measures), by up-skilling or retraining current staff (40%) or by hiring new staff (20%). Often, they combined these various ways of addressing skills (e.g. consultancy services were combined with the retraining of current employees).

Pomorskie is a strong educational centre for the blue economy sectors in Poland. In particular, higher education institutions such as the University of Gdańsk and University of Gdynia have specialised curricula for the blue economy and are increasing their education offer related to the green economy. Nevertheless, skills shortages are already being identified in blue economy sectors and the region has difficulties attracting and retaining talent in research activities. The region currently experiences a high degree of outward migration of highly qualified people, particularly higher education graduates, because of a lack of suitable labour market opportunities. In addition, major challenges have been identified in Pomorskie with the skills ecosystems response to the transition to a greener economy. The collaboration between businesses, research institutions and education providers is particularly weak.

Recommendation: Better anticipate and monitor training needs in relation to the green transition for instance with the participation of the Regional Labour Office and advisory boards. Facilitate the involvement of businesses in the development of training curricula to ensure employers' needs are taken into account (in particular for continuing education and training).

Interviews with stakeholders and the company survey show that the skills ecosystem is only partially responding to the needs of the transition to a greener economy. The response is mainly driven by higher education institutions. The monitoring of skills needs for the green economy transition should be reinforced. This could be the task of the regional Labour Office. This could help identify trends in research, labour market, education requirements and needed qualifications and skills.

Employers also often complain about the quality of training courses developed by public organisations and that the training is not responding to SMEs' needs. Better involving employers and business organisations in the development of curricula could help address these challenges. For instance the London Green Skills partnership is a good example of bringing trade unions, employers, education providers and local authorities together to develop training schemes.

In Pomorskie, the Regional Chamber of Commerce of Pomerania, the Employers of Pomerania, and the Pomeranian Chamber of Crafts for Small and Medium Enterprises could play a more active role in contributing to curricula development, defining specialised training offer especially for SMEs, and delivering some training. The involvement of employers in programme boards or sectorial competencies boards, in accordance with the *Wiedza Edukacja Rozwój na lata 2014-2020* Operational Programme should also be considered.

Recommendation: Help setting up intermediaries to boost business/academia dialogue and foster green innovation. Encourage the promotion of "green values".

This report shows that knowledge sharing within and between sectors, as well as collaboration between academia and businesses are still very limited in Pomorskie. This

> **Box 6.4. The London Green Skills partnership**
>
> In 2011, employers, trade unions, education providers, local authorities and community representatives launched the London Green Skills Partnership, a bottom-up initiative with three main objectives: to create local networks to work together; to provide training, skills and work experience for locals, including the unemployed; and to transform communities into greener, safer, cleaner and more inclusive places.
>
> The partnership is co-ordinated by Unionlearn, a Trade Union body in charge of education and skills, and includes numerous London colleges (e.g. Lewisham, CONEL, South Thames), employers (e.g. Bovis Lendlease, Lakehouse, Carillion), voluntary sector (e.g. Groundwork), Job Centre Plus and trade unions (UCU, UCATT, UNITE). The partnership has developed collaborations between training providers, employers, trade unions, the voluntary sector and communities to deliver sustainability training and employment opportunities.
>
> Activities include training for job seekers in both basic and specific environmental skills needed to transform employment into greener jobs in domains as diverse as retrofitting buildings, hairdressing and waste management. Trained individuals also act as "green ambassadors" in their neighbourhoods and workplaces, sharing their green skills with colleagues and neighbours to foster additional change.
>
> *Source:* Union Learn, 2015; ETUC et al., 2014.

is a major barrier for innovation. There is currently a lack of trust and dialogue between universities and research institutes on the one hand and businesses on the other hand. There is a lack of information flow, often research results or ideas do not reach the business sector and resources could help to bridge this gap. Furthermore, there is a "clash of cultures". In many cases academics are too busy with teaching or research tasks to focus on business interaction. Both groups have very different objectives and cultures, in particular the way information is used for innovation (e.g. open source vs commercially confident).

To overcome this challenge, creating intermediaries between business and research could help as in the case of "innovation connectors" in North East England. The Regional Chamber of Commerce of Pomerania, the Employers of Pomerania, and the Pomeranian Chamber of Crafts for Small and Medium Enterprises may also help create a bridge between the entrepreneurs, science and specialised education.

Skills for the green economy transition can be defined as "the knowledge, abilities, values and attitudes needed to live in, develop and support a sustainable and resource-efficient society" (CEDEFOP, 2012; OECD, 2014a; OECD, 2014b). Building appropriate attitudes and values can be as important as technical skills. Environmental education could play an important role to ensuring a general positive mind-set towards the green economy transition and on ensuring all workers share values and attitudes to support the transition. It could also help to build a talent pipeline, attracting students to careers where shortages have been identified. This could take place thanks to existing projects such as the Hel Marine Station. The Hel Marine Station runs the Blue School project (Błękitna Szkoła), which is aimed at elementary and secondary school students. It offers classes and courses, including field activities, dedicated to marine and coastal ecology.

> **Box 6.5. Creating intermediaries to foster innovation – the example of Innovation connectors in North East England**
>
> Innovation connectors are mainly business clusters and partnerships with a clear geographical and sectoral focus. There are seven innovation connectors in North East England.
>
> Their role is to stimulate economic regeneration, competitiveness and knowledge transfer through innovation across regions. Another goal is to enable the development of world-class facilities and new approaches to integrating businesses and universities and engaging with the community through education. In 2005, the Labour government designed six science cities as innovation connectors: Newcastle upon Tyne, York, Manchester, Nottingham, Birmingham and Bristol. They were envisioned as partnerships between the regional development agency, local authorities, universities and private sector organisations, and their role was to foster innovation and regional development. Part of the rationale for designing these science cities was that the government hoped to promote scientific and research excellence outside the "golden triangle" of London, Cambridge and Oxford.
>
> The research focused on Newcastle Science City, a partnership between the One North East Regional Development Agency, the Newcastle City Council and Newcastle University. Its goal is to create an innovation strategy to stimulate regional economic growth. It has 23 employees working on science business creation, science infrastructure, science networks, education and community. Newcastle Science City aims to position Newcastle globally as a city of science excellence in ageing and health, sustainability and stem cell research. Other goals include creating prosperity for the city and wider region by supporting the creation of new businesses and jobs, assisting existing businesses to innovate and grow, and to ensure that local communities play their part in the development of science. No national funds were used in building these partnerships. It was up to each connector to define and adopt its own model of development, based on existing partnerships and skills. Newcastle Science City's demand-driven model helps entrepreneurs identify their unmet needs and find solutions so they can set up their business in a sustainable way. If an entrepreneur has an idea, experts at Newcastle Science City can help the entrepreneur develop a model and test the idea.
>
> Other important innovation connectors include:
>
> - The National Renewable Energy Centre (Narec), a centre of excellence for delivering world-class innovative technology for new and renewable energy. Its main roles are to support companies within the region looking to invest in energy technologies and supply R&D for the private sector at the regional and national level. Narec is a key national player in the United Kingdom's Low Carbon Industrial Strategy, focused on engineering and industry consultancy. It provides business support services and testing and demonstration facilities for the renewable energy and electrical power sector.
>
> - The North East Technology Park (NETPark) is a science park established to attract businesses through inward investment and to sustain indigenous companies in the region. It provides business support, infrastructure, high-tech, R&D facilities, help finding financial support and networking. NETPark has strong links with the five universities in the region.
>
> - The innovation connector study concluded that there must be an understanding of the specific characteristics and the challenges local businesses face in shaping innovation policy. It also called for raising awareness, improving information sharing and giving universities a wider role in regional and rural development by sharing expertise and facilities.
>
> Role models could be used as examples to encourage other rural businesses to engage actively in regional institutions and programme design.
>
> *Source:* Hubbard and Atterton, 2012.

Leveraging the European Social Fund to encourage employment and skills development

Recommendation: Involve Public Employment Services to help boost green economy skills and prepare career pathways for displaced workers

The report highlights that there is no dedicated programme of Polish Public Employment Services that tackles the skills needed for the green economy. Specific activities to involve both national and regional labour office could be supported by the European Social Fund. For instance, in Flanders, the public employment service (VDAB) plays a large role in promoting skills for the green economy. The Work and Investment plan of the previous Flemish government (2009-2014) gave VDAB the task to develop a long-term strategy on sustainable and green growth, and to introduce sustainability principles in its programmes and course activities. The goal of the strategy was to facilitate changing competences taking into account the changing nature of current technical competences which exist, but also on the development of new, "green", competences. This includes both technical and generic skills. Attention has been given to green activities in VDAB Work Experience Programme (WEP+), aiming at training the long-term unemployed (WSE, 2011).

Recommendation: Encourage and support apprenticeship and training in blue economy sectors

Employers, in particular in the shipbuilding sector, stress that they bear excessively high costs of employing apprentices, even though they receive aid from labour offices for this purpose. The European Social Fund could help reduce the costs of apprenticeship. There are good examples of how to help local companies building a talent pipeline in collaboration with local universities. For instance, the Canadian province of Nova Scotia has developed the Energy Training Programme, a scheme to help SMEs hire post-secondary students in the energy sector. The Energy Training Programme for Students was developed to encourage private-sector employers to hire Nova Scotian post-secondary students for career-related work terms in all sectors of the energy industry. The programme runs every summer and offers employers an opportunity to gain access to students and recent graduates from Nova Scotia universities and community college campuses. A wage subsidy is available for small to medium-sized Nova Scotia companies involved in the energy sector. Eligible companies may receive a 50% wage incentive toward student salaries up to USD 7.50 per hour.

Similarly, there are multiple examples of using the European Social Funds (ESF) to promote green apprenticeships. For instance, in the UK, ESF and Skills Funding Agency funds were secured for the "Heeley City farm's young rangers" project to help 16-18 year olds not in education, employment or training (NEET). The project gave young people lots of engagement in many aspects of animal farming and crop growing, and offered Environmental Conservation Apprenticeships, where participants learnt traditional skills like dry wall building. The awards assessment panel was impressed at the way the project used the environment as a resource to help young people NEET, delivering interesting re-engagement activities for those who prefer practical learning activities.

Furthermore, other aspects could encourage apprentices to remain in the company after they have been trained. Some contractual agreements could require apprentices to remain in the company for a definite period of time after they conclude their education. SMEs could also receive support through wage subsidies to hire technicians that have just completed their education as is the case with Nova Scotia's energy training programme. In addition, courses and training to develop green tourism could be supported. Sailing, yachting, kayaking, surfing, diving, touristic fishing and other active forms of coastal and water tourism should receive support. For example, trainings could be financed by the European Social Funds on interpersonal skills and languages (e.g. English, German, Swedish, Danish or Finnish).

References

Cedefop (2012), *Green skills and environmental awareness in vocational education and training*, European Commission, Luxembourg.

ETUC, BUSINESSEUROPE, CEEP, UEAPME (2014), *Skills Needs in Greening Economies*, (online) http://erc-online.eu/content/uploads/2014/06/Skills-needs-in-greening-economies_FinalReport.pdf(accessed 8 June 2017).

Grøn Omstilling, (2015), *Green Business Development*, (online) https://groenomstilling.erhvervsstyrelsen.dk/green-business-development (accessed 8 June 2017).

Hubbard, C. and J. Atterton (2012), "Unlocking rural innovation in the North East of England: The role of innovation connectors", presentation at the 8th OECD Rural Development Policy Conference held in Krasnoyarsk, Russian Federation, 4 October.

Lewandowski, P. and I. Magda (2014), *Employment in Poland – Labour in the Age of Structural Change*, Warsaw.

OECD (2017), *Boosting Skills for Greener Jobs in Flanders, Belgium*, OECD Publishing, Paris, http://dx.doi.org/10.1787/9789264265264-en.

OECD (2015), *OECD Environmental Performance Reviews: Poland 2015*, OECD Publishing, Paris, http://dx.doi.org/10.1787/9789264227385-en.

OECD (2014a), *Employment and Skills Strategies in the United States*, OECD Publishing, Paris, http://dx.doi.org/10.1787/9789264209398-en.

OECD (2014b), *Employment and Skills Strategies in the Czech Republic*, OECD Publishing, Paris, http://dx.doi.org/10.1787/9789264208957-en.

OECD (2014c), *Innovation and Modernising the Rural Economy*, OECD Publishing, Paris, http://dx.doi.org/10.1787/9789264205390-en.

OECD (2013), *Marine Biotechnology: Enabling Solutions for Ocean Productivity and Sustainability*, OECD Publishing, Paris, http://dx.doi.org/10.1787/9789264194243-en.

OECD (2012), *Linking Renewable Energy to Rural Development*, OECD Publishing, Paris, http://dx.doi.org/10.1787/9789264180444-en.

Union Learn (2015), *Green Skills Partnership*, (online) www.unionlearn.org.uk/green-skills-partnership (accessed 8 June 2017].

WSE (2011), *Naar een groen arbeidsmarktbeleid:een eerste beleidsverkenning*, Departement Werk en Sociale Economie, Vlaamse Overheid, Depotnummer D/2011/3241/128.

ORGANISATION FOR ECONOMIC CO-OPERATION AND DEVELOPMENT

The OECD is a unique forum where governments work together to address the economic, social and environmental challenges of globalisation. The OECD is also at the forefront of efforts to understand and to help governments respond to new developments and concerns, such as corporate governance, the information economy and the challenges of an ageing population. The Organisation provides a setting where governments can compare policy experiences, seek answers to common problems, identify good practice and work to co-ordinate domestic and international policies.

The OECD member countries are: Australia, Austria, Belgium, Canada, Chile, the Czech Republic, Denmark, Estonia, Finland, France, Germany, Greece, Hungary, Iceland, Ireland, Israel, Italy, Japan, Korea, Latvia, Luxembourg, Mexico, the Netherlands, New Zealand, Norway, Poland, Portugal, the Slovak Republic, Slovenia, Spain, Sweden, Switzerland, Turkey, the United Kingdom and the United States. The European Union takes part in the work of the OECD.

OECD Publishing disseminates widely the results of the Organisation's statistics gathering and research on economic, social and environmental issues, as well as the conventions, guidelines and standards agreed by its members.

www.ingramcontent.com/pod-product-compliance
Lightning Source LLC
Chambersburg PA
CBHW082351220526
45470CB00008B/2710